# BLITZ BOY

## AN EVACUEE'S STORY

# BLITZ BOY

## AN EVACUEE'S STORY

ALF TOWNSEND

First published in the United Kingdom in 2008 by
The History Press
The Mill • Brimscombe Port • Stroud • Gloucestershire • GL5 2QG

Reprinted 2009

British Library Cataloguing in Publication Data
A catalogue record for this book is available from the British Library.

ISBN 978-07509-5068-8

Cover illustrations. Front: Evacuees departing London. *(Author's collection)* Back, top: A young Alfie. *(Author's collection)* Bottom: The Archway after the Blitz. *(London Metropolitan Archives)*

Typeset in 11/13.5pt Sabon
Typesetting and origination by
The History Press.
Printed and bound in England.

# CONTENTS

# Wartime Memories

A poem written by my eldest sister Joan, *c.* 1940

I remember the year 1939 – when war broke out, I was only nine
The memories that come flooding back, when the skies were full of enemy
  attacks
The bombs would fall and we would run, to the shelters that weren't much fun
But they kept us safe with God's helping hand – although many fell, never to
  stand
Mum and Dad wanted to keep us safe, so they sent us kids off to a better place
I shall never forget the day we went, so many years ago
And now that I am older, I realise it's the only way they know
But things turned out for the best, we stopped all that running and had a rest
So on our journey we all went many miles away; our eyes were full of tears as
  Mum and Dad had to stay
The lonely times that lay ahead, I used to think when I went to bed
I did my best to fend for us all and prayed each night that Mum would call
And then at last that day did come when we saw our dear, old faithful Mum
The teacher said there is someone outside, so go and dry the tears from your
  eyes
I didn't know what to expect as I went towards the door
There was Mum and Nan and baby brother Ken who was one of us four
I know my prayers were answered by the look on Mum's face
She had to be beside us in this lonely, lonely place
At last my heart was happy just like a bird in song, as Mum said Dad was
  coming and it shouldn't be very long
Oh happy, happy days there would be when at last we became a real family

My eldest sister, Mrs Joan Westmore, returned to Cornwall in her retirement.

# DEDICATION

This book is dedicated to Nicolette, my long-suffering wife of nearly five decades. For many years she had pushed me to write my experiences in the Second World War and, for many years, I chose to continue to live in the comparative comfort of being a well-known, taxi-trade journalist. Finally, I actually wrote three books in the space of four years that were eventually published by Sutton. *Blitz Boy*, about the Second World War, was my first book, followed by *Bad Lads*, my experiences of RAF National Service in the 1950s. My third book entitled *Cabbie*, was a 'warts-and-all' account of my forty-plus years as a London cabby. Strange to relate, but my last book was published first and my first one published last!

My lovely wife Nicolette and my children Nicholas and Joanne, their partners, and all of my seven gorgeous grandchildren, have been my inspiration over the past sad and dreadful years since we lost our wonderful eldest daughter, Jenny. She bravely battled breast cancer for nearly seven years before finally succumbing to this horrid disease over Christmas 1999, at the age of just forty-one.

> Thy Eternal Summer Shall Never Fade
> Our Deepest Love Forever Darling

# INTRODUCTION

I've had this story firmly locked in my brain for over sixty-five years and I thought now was the appropriate time to put it down on paper. Whether my story is published is not really important. What is important is that I can finally purge the demons in my brain that have haunted me for all these years and start to chronicle the events for my children and their children. I believe future generations should know what really happened to many of the inner-city kids during the Second World War, who were unknowingly sent to some Godforsaken hell-holes and had the crap beaten out of them.

Certainly there have been many books and television dramas about evacuees over the years. Quite entertaining for sure, but they all seemed to involve Enid Blyton-type nice, middle-class kids having a spiffing good time in the country on some idyllic farm, with Mummy and Daddy coming down in the car nearly every weekend to visit them. A car, indeed, the most we ever had was a handmade cart with ball-bearing wheels! I remember in the early days of writing this book, the posh old auntie of my daughter's husband showing interest in my story and asking to read my typescript. My daughter had married into the country set who, at one time, lived in the local manor house. They were very nice people, but certainly not like us Londoners. The posh auntie kindly penned a letter to me saying how much she had enjoyed my book. 'But,' she remarked, 'you have got it all wrong about the hardships endured by evacuees.' This was because the evacuees she had housed during the war had a wonderful time and didn't want to go home. That explains what being an evacuee meant in a nutshell – it was a total lottery. Some kids had a great time, while others suffered hell. Yet, that idyllic scenario, penned by some individual from a completely different environment, certainly wasn't like that in my case, or in the case of many other working-class kids. We suffered months and even years of loneliness, hardship, humiliation and in some extreme cases, hatred, physical and mental abuse from the very people who were supposed to be caring for us.

This mass exodus of kids from our major cities in 1940 was unique and the government's hasty organisation programmes left a lot to be desired. It was tantamount to a social revolution and certainly a culture shock for the parochial farmers and middle-class country folk who, whether they liked it or not, were coming into contact with young, frightened, scruffy, somewhat lice-ridden and poverty-stricken kids from the very poorest areas of Britain's cities for the very first time. A large proportion of the people who took in 'Vacs', a derogatory term for evacuees, used by all the local children and many of the adults, did so purely for the cash – I believe it was 8s 3d per week per child, that's just forty-odd pence in new money. It sounds a pittance in today's society but, if you reckoned our boys were fighting on the front line and risking their lives and only earning about £2 per week, it gives you some idea of its spending power. We didn't starve, but by golly we had to earn our corn and in many instances the young lads became almost full-time and unpaid farm labourers. Many of the Cornish farmers certainly showed a very healthy profit on their 8s 3d a week from me and my mates!

Surprisingly, despite my early childhood traumas and the beatings from my so-called 'foster parents', I grew up to be quite a bright kid. I continued my schooling after returning to London when the war ended. I managed to pass the old eleven-plus exam and went on to a decent grammar school. Unfortunately, my aspirations to improve on my early enjoyment of writing at a higher level were thwarted, as in austere post-war Britain my input was badly needed in the minimal family budget. I wasn't unique – far from it, many of my classmates were far more talented than I. But that was the norm for poor families in the late 1940s – especially those like me who had a work-shy father who was at his happiest visiting all the local pubs up the Caledonian Road. To be fair to him, he wasn't exactly work-shy. In those days in the painting and decorating game, the guv'nors held a 'week in hand' when you started a new job. That meant you worked the first two weeks for one week's pay and the other week was held back for when you gave a week's notice to leave. So, if my old Dad was refused a sub (a loan), on his first week's wages, he used to ask for his cards. I think the term he used was: 'I told the guv'nor to lick 'em and stick 'em'. So in effect he often had a new job nearly every week and in many instances, no job at all! My old Dad's proudest moment – and his most profitable – was when I was featured on the sports page of a national evening newspaper and talked of as 'Leyton Orient's big strong, seventeen-year-old centre-forward who could well play for England one day.' My old Dad took a huge bundle of the papers round to all his local pubs and had free beers on the strength of the story for the whole evening and many more after that!

Upon leaving school, I drifted from one menial job to another until doing my National Service in the RAF. After the RAF, my blossoming career as a professional footballer never really took off, simply because I'd had enough of being told what to do and when to do it. Consequently, I always wanted to go out with the lads for a drink and a giggle instead of training. I married the love of my life, Nicolette, in the late 1950s and after becoming the father of our first daughter and our son, I decided in the early 1960s to do 'The Knowledge' and become a London cabbie, a profession I have thoroughly enjoyed for over forty years. The sheer pleasure of writing has always stayed with me and for the past forty years I have been lucky enough to indulge my passion as a hobby. I have edited a trade magazine for many years and written literally hundreds of articles for most of the taxi-trade publications. The majority of cabbies in London all know me by my nickname of 'Alf the Pipe' and unfortunately for them, my ugly mug has been staring out at them from the trade papers every fortnight for the past forty-odd years!

This book has been written following the success of my first two published books *Cabbie* and my second book *Bad Lads: RAF National Service Remembered*, which hit the bookshelves in 2006. Two-and-a-half million young lads like me did National Service and around one million went into the RAF. So my publishers are sweating on a large percentage of that million going out and buying my book!

As far as I am concerned, getting one book published, or, indeed, two or more, is not simply about fame and fortune. I view it as a long-term legacy that my children, their children and their children's children, will enjoy many years after I have kicked the bucket. When a man is blessed with a lovely wife and wonderful children and gorgeous grandchildren, he doesn't need anything else – certainly not money!

*A.E. Townsend*
*Hampstead, 2008*

# ONE

# BEFORE THE WAR

London in the late 1930s wasn't anything like the London we all know today. For a start, it wasn't as cosmopolitan and it had no large ethnic areas. In fact, apart from in the up-market diplomatic circles in Belgravia or the dock areas in the East End, it would have been quite difficult to spot a black person on the streets of our great city. If that rare event happened, all of us kids would run behind the unfortunate person chanting out a rhyme that probably originated way back in the time of the Black Death in 1664. We chanted in unison in the belief that it would bring us good health and keep away the deadly germs. It went thus: 'Touch collar, never swallor, never catch the measles.'

Unlike today, when vast areas of former working-class boroughs have been 'gentrified' by professional people like lawyers, doctors, stockbrokers and architects, simply because of their close proximity to places like the West End, the City or even Canary Wharf, pre-war London was so completely different. It was almost as if an invisible line had been drawn across the capital segregating the 'haves' from the 'have nots'. The 'haves' all had their spacious houses and apartments in places like Mayfair, Belgravia, Kensington, Chelsea, St Johns Wood and Hampstead. While us working-class lot lived our lives, often in abject poverty, in most of the other boroughs. The whole of South London had always been traditionally working-class, as had the East End. Not so today – in Islington, North London, the borough of my birth, house prices are now way beyond the reach of any of the local youngsters wanting to set up home. Back in the 'good old days' when generations of families all lived together in the same street, one of the old aunts or in-laws would always offer a room or two to the newlyweds. Unfortunately, over the next few decades, most of the working-class boroughs would be occupied by professional 'outsiders', the only people who could possibly afford the escalating house prices. I'm not knocking the process, just stating a fact. And the fact is that many of these outsiders literally just use their houses to sleep in. They don't patronise the local shops and they certainly don't use the local markets. But, you frequently see the little green Harrods vans making their deliveries.

It's a bit scary to think that after many hundreds of years of deep-rooted cockney history, this complete transformation of the way that Londoners live has been irrevocably changed in just over half a century! Even now, many thousands of the true cockneys are living on large council estates well outside of London, while their former council properties are being sold off to the highest bidders.

## AND SO TO SCHOOL

One of my earliest recollections is being dragged screaming to the top of our street off Caledonian Road by my Mum, and taken into a little church-like school with a horde of other screaming four-year-olds. I often wonder if I possess an unusual, highly-sensitive, retentive, or photographic memory. I'm always questioning my good friends of my age group about their childhood, but they can't remember anything about being evacuated or even their time in nursery school! I sometimes question if the clarity of my memory is a blessing or a curse!

*Little Alfie with cousin Pat, 1937. (Author's collection)*

*Little Alfie, c. 1936.*
*(Author's collection)*

The smell of that school still lingers in my subconscious after more than sixty-seven years. A damp, musty smell that one always associates with old churches, coupled with the sweet, sickly odour of generations of sweaty little feet doing PE without shoes and socks. These were the days before any deodorants, or daily baths and showers. Once a week, down the old Cally Baths was the norm if you were lucky. If not, it was a ducking with strong carbolic soap in the old tin bath out in the back scullery. This sweet, sickly odour in the school must have permeated the parquet floors over a period of many, many years, because it hung heavy in the air. Our sweaty seat of learning and our old street, Ponder Street, just next to the railway bridge in Caledonian Road, has long since been demolished by the bulldozers after taking a right battering in the Blitz. It has been replaced by one of those many awful council estates typical of town-planning in the 1950s and '60s. I still reckon those old Victorian terraced houses would have lasted much better than these estates!

I distinctly recall this wizened old lady with white hair approaching my Mum with a fixed smile on her face. 'And who have we got here?' she said in a thin, reedy voice. 'This is little Alfie Townsend. Well, he ain't all that little, 'cos he was the heaviest baby born in 1935 in Islington,' Mum said proudly.

'Is that so?' said the wizened old lady with the white hair, with a look of total disinterest on her face. 'So, why are you making that awful noise?' she snapped, grabbing my hand in a vice-like grip. 'If you stop crying little Alfie, we'll put you in the band and you can play music with all the other children.'

She said this all with the same fixed smile on her face. But I was a rotten kid and I didn't want to stay in her smelly old school, or play in her soppy band. So I just carried on yelling and screaming. The next thing I realised was that my Mum and all the other parents had suddenly disappeared and I had had a triangle thrust into my hands, with what looked like a meat skewer to bash it with. The old lady started clapping and we all had to bash our triangles and drums in time with her. The sound was a cacophony of noise, absolutely unbearable and without any semblance of a tune. Then, we were all ordered to sit on the sweaty, smelly floor while she read us a soppy story from a dog-eared book. I was still crying and wanting to go home, so, in a vain effort to shut me up, I was given the job of milk monitor. This entailed carrying in a crate of little bottles of milk and giving one to each of the kids – whether they wanted it or not! I can remember Mum picking me up a few hours later – I was still snivelling. And that's just about the total recollection of my first day of school life.

Yet nursery school didn't last too long for me or my classmates. Something terrible was about to happen. Something so terrible and frightening that we would all remember it to our dying days. Many of my classmates, their parents and their relatives, would perish as tons of high explosives fell on our great city and a generation of young men would fall in the bitter battles to come. Untold millions of innocent civilians would be butchered, simply because they were considered 'undesirables' and didn't comply with the twisted Aryan beliefs of a madman and his bunch of murderous thugs.

This madman was controlling a massive and well-trained fighting force and leading his people into total darkness! The many heroic battles of the Second World War and the Blitz will forever be remembered. But unlike any other conflict in the past, most people will remember it as the war when civilised man turned into a vicious animal and slaughtered more than six million civilians, simply because they were Jewish. The German dictator, Adolf Hitler, had decreed in his twisted mind that it was the

Jewish bankers who had caused Germany's capitulation in the First World War. The German people were desperately searching for a strong man to save their bankrupt economy and they wanted someone to blame for the humiliation of the 1918 Armistice and the loss of so much of their land. Hitler became the man of the moment and conveniently fitted the bill. His rantings against the Jews, the gypsies and any other non-Aryan race were accepted by the gullible German people. This created an open door for the 'Final Solution' and the terrible holocaust that followed in the Nazi death camps. I find it inconceivable that despite innumerable reports from Jewish organisations about the Nazi death camps and gas chambers that the authorities in Britain never really believed it – or rather didn't want to until it became unavoidable. Yet, strangely, these terrible facts seemed to be common knowledge among the ordinary London folk. My old Mum would sometimes threaten me if I was particularly naughty by saying: 'I'll get "Jerry" to put you up the chimney, Alfie.' Surely that's a clear indication of knowing about gas chambers?

The full story of the lack of action by the Allies against the many Nazi death camps may never be known. But the latest evidence about the Second World War seems to indicate that the death camps were situated deep in Poland and originally out of range of Allied bombers. Even after the Allies invaded Normandy and were sweeping across Europe, the decision was taken not to bomb in case they killed all the inmates! In my mind a sad mistake and one the Jews, quite rightly, are still angry about to this day!

## JERRY'S COMING

The faint sound of rumbling in the distance – almost like thunder – was enough to wake me from my childish reverie. I tried in vain to snuggle down under the rough blanket and shut out the sound, but the rumbling got louder and louder and quickly became a mighty roar. I sat up in a blind panic not knowing where I was or what was happening, my heart pounding and my eyes full of tears. Then whoosh! – a blast of warm air hit my cold face and the long, red monster, with the one shiny eye, went hurtling past the platform like an absolute nightmare. Then there was total silence – broken only by my loud snivelling!

This was London during the early days of the Blitz. The 'Phoney War' was over and now the Luftwaffe was pounding London every night. I was one of many thousands of kids and adults trying to sleep in the comparative safety on the platforms of the underground stations. But, as an impressionable five-year-old, the early morning, non-stop train that rushed through the Caledonian Road station used to frighten the living daylights out of me. This fear has never left me and gave me terrible nightmares right through to the early years of my marriage. Even now, when boarding an aircraft, the latent fear expresses itself with clammy hands and feet as the jet engines roar into life and we bump down the runway.

I remember Mum used to say to us kids after school: 'We're all sleeping down the Tube tonight, we've been told that Jerry's coming.' I didn't have a clue who the hell Jerry was. Maybe he was like the insurance man or the 'tally' man who came a-knocking on our door every so often for his money. But, we didn't have to sleep down the Tube when he came round. Mum just used to tell us kids to be very quiet until he got fed up and went away! Then Mum would proceed to busy herself by loading up an old pram with sheets and blankets and all the paraphernalia required to keep four kids happy for the night. Off we'd go from Offord Road, turning right into Roman Way and walking past the dreaded Pentonville prison. I well remember one teatime when we were walking past the ''Ville' – that's what the locals called it – and a stray German bomb had breached the main wall the previous night. Our Dad informed us in his local cockney jargon that 'Sixteen cons had had it away on their toes through the hole.' What the hell are 'cons'? I thought. I didn't have a clue what he was talking about!

Then as soon as we arrived at the Cally Tube, we'd pile into the big, smelly lift, our eyes all big and shiny with excitement as we waited for the whirring sound. Then there were loud screams from all the kids as the lift started descending and we got that funny sinking feeling in our tummies. Then we'd run out when it stopped and dash onto the platform like madmen. It's very difficult to try to describe the scene that greeted my young eyes. In fact, the kids of today just wouldn't believe it – sometimes I don't believe it myself! There were literally hundreds of people on the platform and lots of rickety old double-bunks leaning against the walls. Air-raid wardens in their white tin helmets were shouting out instructions. There were a couple of coppers chatting to people and all the parents were yelling at their kids and telling them to stop making a noise. Some of the older people, like the old boys with their flat caps and wrinkled faces, were just sitting quietly reading their papers and having a puff on their fags.

As the evening wore on, after most of the kids had settled down for the night, the men arrived back from a drinking session in the local pubs. The atmosphere livened up for a while with everyone joining in the singing of all the old cockney pub songs and music hall numbers. What fascinated me was the fact that most everyone knew ALL the words of ALL the songs! Fair enough, even I knew some of the words of 'Maybe It's Because I'm a Londoner'. But everybody knew the words of such weird songs as 'The Biggest Aspidistra in the World' and 'When Father Painted the Parlour You

Couldn't See Him for Dust'. The final song was always a rousing rendition of the classic 'I'm 'Ennery the Eighth I Am'. The words are still implanted in my subconscious.

> I'm 'Ennery the Eighth I am, 'Ennery the Eighth I am, I am
> I got married to the widow next door, she's been married seven times
>   before
> And every one was a 'ennery, not a 'arry, or a Willy, or a Sam
> I'm her eighth ol' man called 'ennery, 'ennery the Eighth I am

But, when the eerie wail of the sirens started, sounding for all the world like a demented soul in torment, it all went deathly quiet – even the boozy mob suddenly sobered up. Then came the deep drone of the aircraft, the sound of the ack-ack guns and the thud of bombs hitting the ground. Thinking back to those harrowing times, I often shudder to think what would have happened if the station had suffered a direct hit, as did the unfortunate Balham station in South London. Nobody really knows how many perished simply because nobody knew how many people were down there at the time. The story was the same at other terrible tragedies of the Blitz, like the school in Agate Street in the East End. Originally more than 600 people had been shipped there by coaches, supposedly taking them away to safety after their homes had been flattened by the hordes of German bombers. For sure, the school had a concrete roof but it was still far too close to the docks. Thankfully, after the first night, half of them had been shipped elsewhere. Sadly, the following night the school received a direct hit, the bomb literally cutting the school in half on impact, exploding inside and killing many innocent souls. One half of the building then slid into the crater before the rescue teams arrived. They started digging and putting body parts into rubble baskets, then loaded their gory cargo into ambulances along with intact bodies. The local swimming baths had been drained of water and used as a temporary mortuary and the gory cargo was unloaded and hosed down. The mortuary attendants were left trying desperately to match the body parts in a nightmare jigsaw puzzle. Horribly, there were all kinds of bits and pieces left over. The official death toll was recorded as just seventy and they were buried in a mass grave before the scene was concreted over. Nobody knew how many had died because, again, nobody really knew how many people were in the school on that terrible night. Locals believe more than 200 perished with generations of the same families being completely wiped out.

It was the same horrific story in Bermondsey close to the wharves in Tooley Street. One of the railway arches in Druid Street had been sandbagged on both sides and converted into a shelter. Someone had got a piano inside and everyone was having a jolly-up on a Friday night, 25 October 1940 – the shelter was packed out. Suddenly, a large bomb went straight through the railway line and penetrated the shelter from above before exploding inside it. Again, nobody really knew how many poor souls were inside in the first place because many had simply just walked in off the street. Even so, the official death toll was listed at only seventy-seven. Rumours swept around London during the Blitz that the various council depots were stacked high with many thousands of coffins. These rumours were in fact correct. In 1937, the Air Ministry had estimated that the probable terrible outcome of some 600 tonnes of bombs falling on the city would result in 20,000 casualties.

Thankfully, what the authorities hadn't predicted was the large numbers of displaced people who had been made homeless by the savage bombing. So, the 600 tonnes of bombs dropped on 7 September 1940 only caused about one-tenth of the estimated 20,000 or so casualties. As for us, we were only half a mile up the road from the prime German targets of Euston, Kings Cross and St Pancras stations and the giant gasometers. The Luftwaffe pilots were quite happy to shed their bomb loads if they couldn't quite reach their targets. So, our area of London took a right pasting nearly every night and for many nights until the end of the Blitz.

Early the next morning, it was pack up all your things and walk the return journey back home. I well remember the smell of London after an air raid. It smelt like when Dad made a big fire in the garden to burn all the old wood. And there was this strange glow in the early morning sky, a bit like the sun, but not. During the daylight hours, us local kids used to scour the streets for shrapnel, especially after we saw the dogfights in the sky between the British and German planes. The most prized possessions to swap were any pieces with German writing on them – most prized of all and worth child-like fortunes were those pieces that had part of the black German cross or the swastika! With a piece like that, you were the local king! Other less fortunate kids were often maimed and even killed by picking up unexploded bombs and grenades.

After countless nights of sleeping down the Cally Tube, things started to change. One day a gang of men arrived at our house with big curved sheets of corrugated iron. Then they started to dig a large, deep oblong hole in our garden. With all the kids watching in fascination, the workmen proceeded to place the sheets of corrugated iron over the big hole, just like putting on a roof. Finally, they shovelled the earth from the hole back over the corrugated iron. I remember hearing one of the old girls say, knowingly, but still chillingly, in between puffing her fag: 'Oh yus, these 'ere Anderson shelters are blast-proof and you'll only cop it with a direct hit from Jerry'. But sleeping in the Anderson shelter was much more fun and not half as scary as sleeping down the Tube. And we only had to walk down to the bottom of our garden when the siren started. My two sisters shared one of the rickety double bunks and me and my Mum, holding our baby brother, shared the other. I believe later in the Blitz, some bright spark designed another sort of shelter and called it the Morrison shelter. It consisted of a collapsible steel frame that fitted over the kitchen table. This, I am told, was the theory: when the sirens sounded, all the family had to get under the kitchen table, which protected them from the blast. I don't think anyone had bothered to work out what would happen to the people under the kitchen table if they suffered a direct hit and the house collapsed. Or, what about those poor souls on the top floors of council flats? But the Anderson shelters were very basic and always very damp, with water falling down the side walls and lots of creepy-crawlies all over the floor. It was the dank, earthy smell that used to upset me, a bit like lying alive in a coffin, I suppose. That smell has never left me to this very

*Alfie's Dad, who served between the wars. (Author's collection)*

day. Sleeping in an Anderson shelter most nights was probably extremely unhealthy for both young, under-nourished kids with breathing problems and grown-ups alike. But, it helped our family to survive. Many's the time we came out of the shelter in the early morning after a very heavy air raid, blinking from the sun's rays and seeing scenes of utter devastation, with whole streets razed to the ground. I recall once when one of our neighbours copped a direct hit and the house looked just like a flattened pile of rubble. I overheard our Mum say to a friend, knowingly pointing at the rubble. 'She ain't bleedin' taking the mickey out of our Anderson shelter now, is she?'

But the air raids got progressively worse and more prolonged, as more and more German bombers battered London every night. It seemed we spent nearly every night down in our shelter. Our Mum was adamant, she used to say: 'Your Dad and his boozy mates are big enough and ugly enough to make up their own minds where they want to sleep. But my kids go down the shelter.' Suddenly, the German bombers became so confident that they started coming in the daytime. London's air defences and its ack-ack batteries were being overwhelmed and the sky seemed to be always full of wave after wave of German planes from dawn until dusk. Records from the war show that London was bombed continuously for fifty-seven consecutive nights, with 42,000 civilians killed and some 45,000 injured. Hitler's right-hand man, Hermann Goering, had managed to convince the Führer that he could destroy both London and the RAF to clear the way for a German invasion of England. But as history tells us, he got it wrong. The Luftwaffe failed to break the civilian morale with their terror-bombing and, more crucially, because of the RAF's early-warning radar system, they failed to destroy our air force. Hitler had duly made the worst military decision of what, until then, had been a string of brilliant successes. He decided instead on Operation Barbarossa, the attack on the USSR.

Something drastic had to happen to me or I probably wouldn't be here telling my story today. Evacuation to the country for all the city kids was the number one priority for the government. Sadly, many of these kids – mostly from London – were unknowingly sent out of the frying pan into the fire. When the Luftwaffe suddenly switched their targets the following year, places like Coventry, the Midlands and Plymouth, which were originally designated as 'safe areas', took a terrible hammering with great loss of life. How ironic to be uprooted from your home and family, dragged to another part of the country, then meet an untimely death in a strange city! As for me, like any other young boy, I was in a world of my own. For sure, I used to get scared, but I was too young to really understand the seriousness of our situation. It was all a bit of a lark to me,

*Alfie's sisters, Joan and Irene. (Joan Westmore's collection)*

sleeping down the Tube and in the Anderson shelter and collecting bits of German aeroplanes. I can recall looking intently into the faces of some of the grown-ups and recognising the fear they were trying to control. But, my young mind couldn't relate to the dangers and really comprehend what they were frightened about!

Through no choice of my own, my great country adventure that was to last nearly five years, was beginning to unfold.

# TWO

# MUM SAYS IT'S A TRIP TO THE SEASIDE

My two sisters and myself – my little brother was too young – were told by our Mum, as Dad was away working, that we were all going on a train down to the seaside for a lovely little holiday. I can always remember our Mum cuddling me and tearfully telling us: 'Bleedin' Jerry won't be able to get you down there, will 'e?' By now,

*Crossing Holloway Road on the way to the country. (Author's collection)*

*Evacuees on their way. (London Metropolitan Archives)*

I knew that Jerry were the people responsible for dropping bombs on us every night. But where on earth 'down there' was, I hadn't the faintest idea!

Our battered old suitcases were packed and, if I had been older and wiser, I would have realised immediately that nobody ever took ALL their worldly possessions for a 'lovely little holiday'! We carefully carried our Mickey Mouse gasmasks and had huge brown labels pinned to our coats with our names and address printed on them. We took the same walk down Roman Way, past the prison to the Cally Tube. Down in the big lift and out on to the same scary platform where we used to sleep – still in a mess with the old double bunks lying around. Now the platform was completely empty, but I only had to shut my eyes to get a clear vision of all those hundreds of petrified people with utter fear on their faces, all staring upwards and listening to the bombs exploding. I started to twitch in blind panic as I felt the blast of hot air in my face and the train seemed to burst into the station. Even today, I still twitch nervously when the 'big red monster' with the 'one staring eye' comes rushing scarily into the station and I swear I sometimes can still visualise those old double bunks and those frightened faces many years later!

We finally arrived at a very crowded Paddington station and, from my low vantage point halfway down to the floor, the whole place was an absolute madhouse. Hundreds of people were milling around, all dressed in uniforms and all carrying kitbags. There were soldiers, sailors and the blue of the RAF. Some even had black faces with big, bushy beards and they wore funny turbans on their heads. All the pushing and all the shoving and all the noise suddenly became too much for me and I started

*Evacuees at their country school. (London Metropolitan Archives)*

*Evacuees all packed up and ready to go. (London Metropolitan Archives)*

to cry. Suddenly, a big warm hand was placed on my head and I heard a deep voice saying: 'What's the matter with you, little fella?' I looked up through my tears and saw this huge man dressed in an RAF uniform and sporting the biggest moustache I'd ever seen. I snivelled in reply, cuffing my nose with my sleeve in the process: 'I don't like all this noise mister and I wanna go home.' He squatted on his knees in front of me and holding my hands very gently, he said: 'We all want to go home little fella, but we've all got a job to do, even you.' With that, he reached into his pockets and pulled out a coin. 'See this little fella?' he smiled, waving this silver coin in front of my face. 'Everybody who volunteers to fight for King and Country gets the King's shilling', he said, pressing the coin into my wet, sticky hand. 'So here's the King's shilling for you little fella, you are now one of the soldiers of the King. So be brave and keep your chin up.' Then

*Off the bus and onto the train. (London Metropolitan Archives)*

he was gone, even before my Mum had a chance to see him disappearing into the heaving horde. Consequently, she never did believe my story of how I managed to obtain a silver shilling and always called me a 'fibber' for years. Moments of kindness like that live long in your memory. I had no idea what on earth he was talking about but, as a scared kid, I knew this total stranger was going out of his way to show his empathy. I often wonder if he made it through the war and went home to his family again. He was such a lovely man and he deserved to survive.

Suddenly, a big-chested lady in a green uniform came up to my Mum. Even to this very day I can still get the smell of her in my senses. A strong flowery perfume, coupled with an overpowering odour of carbolic soap. 'And your name my dear?' she enquired in a funny posh voice that I hadn't heard before. My Mum gave her the names of us three kids and

'Mrs Green Uniform' began flicking through her list. 'Oh yes, here we are,' she said, ticking off our names on her list. 'Would you please go to that lady over there?' pointing in the direction of another green-uniformed woman who was surrounded by a crowd of kids. 'She is in charge of your carriage', she muttered, consulting her list and scribbling down some notes. Again, more name-taking and more peering down at our brown labels by other Green Uniforms followed. 'You boy, stand over there and let your sisters stand over here', said one of them. Then, across came another lady with 'scrambled-egg' on her hat, clearly denoting a senior officer. All the other Green Uniforms smartly saluted her and she promptly proceeded to put us back in line where we had originally started! Okay, so they WERE volunteers, but it WAS a shambles!

*Take the cat as well! (London Metropolitan Archives)*

*Evacuees leaving London. (Author's collection)*

Eventually, after lots of shouting and screaming, our group was all rounded up. We kissed Mum goodbye and clambered happily aboard the train. I can't honestly remember crying when the train pulled out of the station. Why should I? It was a great adventure, I was with my two sisters and Mum had said she was coming down to see us in a couple of days. So, I just stood at the window with loads of other kids, waving our arms like mad at all the cameras that were photographing us. These were early days in the war and we were of great media interest. Pictures of the smiling kids were great propaganda for the government's future evacuation plans. With the benefit of hindsight, many of the evacuees – me included – would have welcomed a follow-up from the authorities after we'd settled in. That would certainly have alleviated an awful lot of heartache for all those kids like me and many years of horrific nightmares!

The journey to the seaside was pretty grotty. The train was packed to the roof with thousands of screaming kids and flustered service personnel. All I can remember is sitting on my old battered suitcase out in the corridor, right next to an evil-smelling toilet that was in constant use. The ladies in the blue of the RAF were very kind and friendly to me, giving me a cheery 'hello' every time they went by. But the army boys started to get a bit rowdy and raucous after drinking lots of beer. I recall, after a long time of steaming at full speed through the beautiful countryside, the train starting to slow down. I stood up and peered out of the window and was fascinated to see we were passing a beach and near enough to the sea to almost touch it. I found out many years later that his was in fact part of Brunel's Great Western Railway masterpiece at Dawlish in Devon. Bypassing all the hills and the mountains helped save money on the engineering costs. The train picked up speed again and, after all that free lemonade and cheese sandwiches, the queue of kids waiting to use the foul-smelling toilet got bigger and bigger! Again, for some unknown reason, we slowed almost to a halt and there were funny clanking noises coming from underneath the train. I rushed to the window with all the other kids to see what was happening and got the fright of my young life. We were chugging ever so slowly across a gigantic bridge that stretched as far as the eye could see. And, looking down many hundreds of feet to the water below was really scary. I could see lots of warships anchored there, all shapes and sizes, but they all looked so tiny. One of the soldiers told me that this was the famous Saltash Bridge near Plymouth that separated Devon from Cornwall – yet another engineering feat by Brunel. I've seen many breathtaking sights in my life since then but that bridge was something else – so huge and so imposing. But little did the good people of Plymouth realise that they would soon be getting an unwelcome visit from Hermann Goering's Luftwaffe in the very near future and that their docks would get a pasting with many civilian casualties. Sadly, some of the fatalities were evacuees from London who had been shipped down to Plymouth.

The train started to pick up speed and the regular, repetitive track sounds of 'de-dah-de-dah, de-dah-de-dah, de-dah-de-dah', plus the swaying of the coaches, eventually made me nod off because I was quite content. I had never seen real cows or sheep before, or even green fields. This was a super adventure with my two sisters.

My sleep was fitful and troubled, with the whole of my young life flashing across my brain – almost like a giant cinema screen. I could smell the sickly, sweet aroma of the sweaty parquet floor in my first nursery school and my Mum running off and leaving me with that horrible old lady. This was followed by the excitement and fear of sleeping down the Tube and being petrified by the empty train rushing through in the early hours, not really knowing what was going on. Then there was the acrid smell of burning buildings and the dank, earthy smell of the Anderson shelter. Was it just a bad dream and had it never really happened?

Suddenly, a man's stentorian voice on a crackling loudspeaker woke me from my fitful reverie. 'Pa-r-rr, this be Pa-r-rr,' boomed a voice in a strange accent. 'Change 'ere for Lux–u-ly-an, Bu-gle, Roche, St Col-umb Road, Quintr-ell Downs and New-kay.' My big sister grabbed my suitcase and my hand and shouted: 'Look sharp Alfie or we'll get left behind.' Then, it was sheer pandemonium as hundreds of screaming kids left one train and made a bee-line for the other train on the far side of the platform. All the ladies in green uniforms were fighting a losing battle. They were shouting out for order and safety, but it was the first ones on the new train who got a seat. So their loud shouts of 'Wait for me' and 'slow down' fell on deaf ears. We managed to grab a seat and leant back in triumph. Little did any of us know that the remainder of the journey was only about an hour down the line and hardly time for a chat!

## ARRIVING AT THE SEASIDE

As we chugged into a station, I heard someone say that we were now in Cornwall. But what did I know? The farthest I had ever been in my young life was an afternoon out at Highbury Fields and the only interesting things to see there were the massive barrage balloons that supposedly stopped low-flying German aircraft. I found out when I was much older that barrage balloons and ack-ack guns were not much more than a token gesture and almost totally ineffectual!

It was absolute bedlam getting off the train. Lots of pushing, shoving and screaming and crying – while the big ladies in green uniforms fluttered about shouting in attempts to keep their groups together. I was safe and secure, tightly clutching my big sister's hand. We filed out of the station to be greeted by more ladies, all wearing green uniforms. They started pushing up to us kids and peering at our brown labels, while in the background I could see a row of dirty grey charabancs – or coaches, as they are called nowadays. After what seemed like an eternity, our 'chara' was full up with screaming kids and the inevitable big ladies in green uniforms. So, off we went down the pretty country lanes with all the kids making a terrible racket and larking about. Within a few minutes the chara stopped and the driver yelled out in a funny accent. 'This be Primrose Farm, missus.' The big lady holding the clipboard looked down her list and motioned to the two little girls sitting in front of me saying. 'Will the Smithson gells please follow me?' So, off they toddled holding hands and when the clipboard lady came back we started off again with a grinding of gears and a jerk forward. This pattern of start and stop, with

*It wasn't all like this! (Author's collection)*

the driver calling out all the funny names in a funny accent and the big lady with the clipboard calling out the names of the kids carried on until there were only a dozen kids left on board with me and my two sisters. I wasn't too upset when my youngest sister's name was called out. She gave us both a big hug and said she would come round to see us soon. Absolute blind panic gripped my young, confused mind when we next stopped outside a pretty white stone farmhouse and my big sister's name was called. The realisation finally dawned in my young brain that I was going to be separated from my big sister who always looked after me. I was to be sent to a strange place all on my own. I went absolutely berserk in my blind panic, grabbing my big sister in a vice-like grip and screaming like a mad thing. I yelled pitifully: 'Please don't take my Joanie away from me.' She started crying and held me tight saying: 'Don't worry Alfie, I'm only up the road from you.' But no way would I let go of her. I shouted and

I screamed and kicked out in all directions, using the foulest language I knew – even when the driver helped the big lady pull us apart. I distinctly remember the driver's voice in the background saying to the lady in the green uniform with some concern. 'This bain't be right m'dear, you'm splitting up the little fella from his big sister, he be just a baby.'

'My dear fellow,' she snapped back at him, while clutching tightly on to my big sister. 'There happens to be a war on and everyone has to suffer some discomfort.'

The last glimpse I had of my big sister through tear-filled eyes was when the chara pulled away. She was waving like mad and standing next to a kind-looking, grey-haired woman. It really was an absolute lottery when you were evacuated. The couple who took in my big sister grew to love her as their own and pleaded with my Mum later on to let them adopt her. Unknowingly, I had drawn the short straw and was heading for a hell-hole with a witch in charge. In life, you win a few and you lose a few, but that's the luck of the draw!

# THREE

# PENRYN PURGATORY

I was sobbing inconsolably for the rest of the journey. The dull sound of the driver's voice calling out the destinations seemed like a bad dream. Suddenly, the chara stopped and through my teary haze I saw the big lady in the green uniform heading purposely towards me. 'Come along young chappie,' she said, with a fixed smile on her face. 'Your new auntie is waiting to say hello to you.' 'I ain't bloomin' going anywhere without my sister,' I screamed like a mad person. 'I've 'ad enough of the stupid seaside and I wanna go 'ome to my Mum.' She let out a sigh of exasperation. 'Don't be so tiresome,' she said, getting a hold of me, 'it's been a very long day and we're all extremely tired.' With that, she dragged me kicking and screaming out of the chara. I still remember the driver kindly saying: 'It won't be for long little fella and then you can go home.'

It must have been winter, because I felt freezing cold standing outside the chara. The silence of the countryside, apart from my snivelling, was broken by the sound of a woman's loud voice with a strong accent saying: 'Who be making them noises like the beasts in the fields?' I looked up to see a very old, very thin woman with tied-back grey hair and piercing blue eyes, staring out at me angrily through funny steel-rimmed glasses. She grabbed my hand roughly and said in a quiet, threatening voice: 'We'll have no more of this silly noise my boy. Just you'me pick up that-there bag and you can wash your face before supper.' With that, I was dragged screaming into a very dark house out of sight of the lady in the green uniform who hadn't even bothered to come in and check me out. I was dumped into a very dark bedroom and just left to cry myself to sleep, freezing cold and starving hungry from lack of food and frightened half to death.

The next morning I woke up after a restless night, still freezing cold and hungrier than ever. I looked around at what would be my home for God-only-knew how long. Just about every single thing in my tiny room was tatty and dirty. The once-white lace curtains at the grubby windows, now took on the appearance of a light, sooty grey, finely peppered with years of bird feathers and droppings. The birds obviously used this particular window ledge for courting and to preen themselves every spring. The sparse furniture in the room, including an antiquated wardrobe and an even more antiquated dressing-table, could be described in today's parlance as 'rough-country rustic'. And, when I say 'rough' I mean VERY rough! Even my bed, with its rough-hewn ornamental headboard, looked as though it had been carved in anger by a mad Cornishman after a gutful of cider! The wobbly unit in the corner was obviously my 'bathroom', a chipped jug and wash basin – full of freezing cold water, just the job for a winter's morning! My 'bijou' toilet facilities consisted of a battered tin potty under the bed on a moth-eaten carpet that must have been running alive with bugs! The whole room smelt of damp, a bit like the Anderson shelter in our garden back in London. The tearful inspection of my 'cell' was rudely interrupted by a woman's loud voice with a strong accent shouting out 'You boy' – that was to be my name for the duration of my stay. 'Get yourself washed in the basin and come down for your porridge – and look sharp about it.' I did as I was instructed in the freezing cold water and went down the stairs following the smell of food into the kitchen. My tormentor was there, the skinny old woman with the funny glasses and the piercing blue eyes. Sitting next to her was an ugly, podgy boy, a couple of years older than me. I didn't like the look of him from the start and I was right to be suspicious. This was 'Young Sidney', the offspring of the Witch and her husband and, as it turned out farther down the line, he was a right plonker. 'Sit you down there boy,' said the Witch.

'Eat your porridge, go to the outside lavvy, then my Sidney will kindly take you to school.' So, I walked with Sidney to my new school for God knows how far – it certainly took us a good half an hour each way and Sidney wasn't in the least bit interested in talking to me. And the teacher wasn't the slightest bit interested in teaching vacs; he knew full well we would all be moving on. And, as for me, I wasn't the slightest bit interested in mixing with the tight-knit Cornish kids. They didn't want the likes of me there and I didn't want to be there either. So, I just sat at the back of the class totally oblivious of what was being taught. Playtimes became a bit of a problem for starters, especially when the brother of the gang-leader of the class decided to dig me out one day in front of a crowd of kids, just because I was a vac.

He starting taunting me in front of his mates and saying diabolical things like. 'I do think that your Ma and Pa 'ave been blown up by them-there bombs.' Anyway, after I had given him a smack on the gob and made his nose bleed, the others hinted that I was in dead trouble because his brother 'Big Dennis' would be coming to sort me out! Anyway, Big Dennis arrived with a couple of his minders in the afternoon play break.

I might have been a youngster but I was streetwise and I knew my way around the block. I knew exactly what was coming, so I had 'borrowed' a large spanner from the garden shed and tucked it down my trousers. Funny that, I wonder why the two minders 'bottled out' when I brandished it up their nostrils! As for Big Dennis, he was just a big old softie and told me his brother was a pain in the arse and got what he deserved. We became good mates for the rest of my stay.

The return walks back to the Witch were much the same. Sidney had been lumbered with me and I had been lumbered with him. The dislike was mutual. But he was a little wary of me, even though he was bigger and older. He'd heard on the school grapevine that I had bloodied someone's nose and become good mates with one of the school heavies. On top of that, the frustration of my predicament, coupled with my utter dislike of my situation, made me very feisty and likely to throw him some serious verbals. In fact, one time I threatened to break his legs if he grassed me up to his Mum for doing something which was forbidden. I hated my predicament and I hated just about everyone around me. Even as youngster I was still proud to be a London lad from the Angel and determined that these 'carrot crunchers' weren't going to grind me down.

It's very difficult to estimate just how long I suffered at the hands of that awful woman in Penryn. It seemed like an eternity, but it was possibly only one winter. I can remember walking to school every day in the thick snow with the Witch's son; then coming back from school, still walking in the thick snow. My mind recalls passing crossroads that had a petrol station on the corner. Many years later, I became a fan of the American artist Edward Hopper and was drawn into buying a huge print of one of his famous paintings called 'The Gas Station', simply because it looked exactly like the petrol station at that crossroads. My daily orders were to go into the woods on my way back from school and bring in some small twigs for the fire – or kindling as the Witch called it. Only me, mind you, not her fat, horrible son. Because I didn't have any kind of gloves or protection for my hands, or even waterproof shoes, this caused me to get severe chilblains on my fingers and toes. Then, she tried teaching me to tie my shoe laces with a bow. But, because of my weeping chilblains and my swollen fingers, I couldn't do a bow. So, I was punished and locked in a decrepit outside woodshed until, as she so succinctly put it: 'You'me learn to obey your elders.'

That woodshed was a nightmare. It was situated downwind, next door to the outside privy, and the attendant noxious smells came wafting in at all times of the day or night. I suppose it was about twice the size of a telephone box with logs piled up to the roof and a small space near the door where I sat on a rickety old chair, sobbing my heart out. It wasn't quite so scary in the daylight hours because I could see the sky through the gaps in the wood. But I was absolutely petrified at being locked in there at night. Someone had thrown an old army-issue blanket over all the tools lying on the floor and I can still recall the red 'WD' stamped on it. So when it was freezing cold – which seemed like the whole time – I'd pick up the old army blanket, shake out all the spiders and ants, then wrap it around me and sit on the rickety old chair and just cry.

My terror of the darkness in the woodshed led to bed-wetting and instead of realising that I was a frightened, lonely young chap, who was missing his family, this paragon of Cornish virtue threw me into the woodshed yet again for my 'misdemeanors'. The nightmares and fear of the dark stayed with me into the early years of my marriage. My wife often tells the kids the story about the time I rugby-tackled her late at night when she was heading for the toilet and heavily pregnant. Or of the time when I jumped out of bed in a blind panic, tied our posh Venetian blinds into hideous shapes – not your modern-day plastic ones mind you, but tough aluminium blinds painted in pretty colours – smashed the window with one violent punch and dived out onto the lawn. Luckily for me, it was a ground floor flat!

You couldn't, in all honesty, describe my adopted home in Penryn as a farm. I suppose a small-holding would be a fair description, albeit a very run-down and ramshackle affair. It's funny what the brain stores in its memory bank for years, isn't it? But I can't honestly remember much about the husband of the house, 'Uncle Sid'. He was a dead ringer for his son: fat, rude and ugly. I can't ever remember him speaking to me during my stay – even while I was helping him pen the pigs, or bringing in the cows, or collecting the chickens' eggs. He was a big, chunky man with a rosy complexion – it could have been the booze – and he always wore a battered old flat cap and forever had a fag-end in his mouth. But what fascinated me about his fag-ends was that they were never, ever alight. He must have been rolling his own with cow dung or the like! His way of speaking was just a grunt or two and a finger pointed at what he wanted me to do. It was the same over the dinner table on the very rare occasions that I was allowed to eat with the family. Then, he'd just get up when he'd finished eating, rudely emit a loud burp, and walk out without a word to anyone. We'd hear the front door crash a minute later and that was him down the local village pub for the night with all his farmer friends. I often used to be laying still awake in bed and still freezing cold when he came back from the pub well into the night. By that time and with all the booze in him, he was full of Dutch courage and would stand up to the Witch and give her back as much as he got.

'What time you'me call this Sidney?' she would yell out loudly. 'Oye calls this after closing time and that be the end of the matter,' he would slur in reply. 'Well,' she would yell back, 'it b'aint be the end of the matter with me. You're a drunken bugger, just like your father and your brothers.' Then Uncle Sid would really go off on one with the help of the booze. His voice rose to a crescendo and you could hear him bash his fist against the wardrobe. 'Is that so?' he yelled. 'My bloody so-called drunken father and brothers were sober enough to tell me not to marry you, them always did say you were no bloody good. Them did say I'd be better off with a sheep or a cow.'

Now it was open warfare and Uncle Sid had gone over the top with that remark. Suddenly, there was the sound of a loud, solid bang and a yell of anguish from Uncle Sid. 'What d'ya wanna hit me with that there chamber pot for?' he screamed out in terror. 'You'me just get into that bed this minute, you drunken bugger,' snarled the Witch, 'or you'me be getting another whack somewhere you won't like.' Then there was the sound of the bed creaking as poor old Uncle Sid got in and surrendered the argument. Then, peace and quiet, with just the sound of the wind gently blowing through the trees and casting shadows across my window. I just chuckled to myself as I settled down for the night. Even with a bellyful of booze, poor old Uncle Sid still couldn't win an argument with the Witch and he never would!

*A scruffy Alfie, pre-war.*
*(Author's collection)*

With the passing of time and the benefit of hindsight, I now realise that my sporadic invitations to the family dinner table just happened to coincide with the sporadic visits from one of the ladies in green uniforms. The Witch wasn't daft, she was mean and cunning. She made doubly sure her evacuee money of 8s 3d a week wasn't jeopardised. At the outset and long before I discovered what a cold-blooded pig he was, I felt quite sorry for poor old Uncle Sid. It was painfully obvious, even to a young nipper like me, who wore the trousers in this household. The spiteful Witch was the guv'nor and Uncle Sid kept quiet and did her bidding, just to keep the peace.

I recall with horror one fine morning when she said to me: 'You boy!' (I still didn't have a name with her), 'go and fill up that bucket with water, take it out to Uncle Sid in the barn and tell him to take care of those bloody kittens right away.' How exciting, I thought in my innocence. We've got some new kittens and I'm going to help wash them. The four newborn baby kittens were lying on the floor of the barn looking very cosy on the straw and snuggling up to their mother's tummy. 'Can I hold one please, Uncle Sid?' I said. He grunted in his normal manner and shook his head and then, to my absolute horror and disbelief, he picked up the kittens one by one and proceeded to drown them in the bucket without showing the slightest flicker of emotion. Just puffing away on his unlit dog-end and grunting as he held them under the water. It was almost as if he was just doing the washing-up. My distraught screams and shouts of protest brought the Witch rushing to the barn. No sympathy for me, and yet again I was given a clump around the ear, thrown into the dark woodshed as a punishment, without my supper yet again.

As a city kid, I had a lot to learn about life on a farm and the cruel way many of the farmers used to treat their livestock. In my childish brain, the cows, pigs and the hens were like pets to me. Not so to Uncle Sid: many was the time I watched in utter horror and disbelief as he punched and kicked the cows and the sheep. And what was their 'crime'? Well, according to my good Uncle Sid, they were 'lazy buggers'. The Witch instructed me one day to go out and tell Uncle Sid that she wanted a big, fat chicken. I duly obeyed her order and followed Uncle Sid to where the chickens were clucking about, totally oblivious of what this red-faced monster was going to do. He strolled among the chickens looking them over, picking one up and squeezing it in the tummy and putting it down again. Suddenly, he grabbed one by the neck with his big, beefy hands and almost casually – as if he was ringing out a wet cloth – he wrung the wretched bird's neck. The poor old chicken who had been clucking away and eating its food just seconds before let out one loud squawk before expiring. That wasn't the end of the horror. Uncle Sid grunted loudly, puffed on his unlit dog-end, looked up and attempted to pass me the still-warm corpse of the chicken to carry back to the Witch. I just ran off in horror screaming like a mad thing. Needless to say, I had to pay again for my disobedience with another spell in my prison.

To be fair to the rest of the country people, it wasn't all doom and gloom in Penryn. I loved the beautiful countryside, I loved the animals and I loved being with them. I especially enjoyed some of the jobs that were allocated to me like feeding the lovely, fat old pigs and making clucking noises when feeding the chickens. My very first job before breakfast was to return the huge milk churns to the cowshed. Now, in those far-off days, every farm or smallholding had a wooden platform outside the front gate. It was built exactly to the same height as the milk lorry that called every morning. The milk guy used to back alongside the wooden platform, load the full churns and replace them with empties. And it was my job to waggle them down the wooden steps and spin them up the muddy path to the cowshed. I can't really explain why, but I thoroughly enjoyed wheeling the milk churns into the cowshed and saying a friendly 'good morning' to the three old cows. Mind you, cows are lovely, gentle animals. For sure, they can be a bit on the dopey side but they're never aggressive. I recall being so upset one morning when I breezed into the cowshed to say good morning and saw Buttercup, the old cow, laying on the ground, with her feet up in the air. Even I knew something serious had happened and my frantic calls brought Uncle Sid a-puffing up the path. He looked down at the stricken animal and for once in his life he spoke to me, muttering those immortal and 'sympathetic' words. 'Bugger that cow, it's going to cost me a pretty penny to replace her'.

Later in the day a lorry arrived with some lifting gear on board. Poor old Buttercup was attached to the cable, then dragged unceremoniously from the cowshed and hoisted on to the lorry. That was that. A short trip down to the knacker's yard to make more food for all the fat pigs and life went on as before!

I'll give the country folk their fair due – they did stick together and help each other in times of need. One day I noticed the Witch was doing a lot of cooking and baking and I overheard her talking to a neighbour and managed to grasp the gist of the conversation. It seemed that one of the local farmers had tragically lost his wife during childbirth. He was absolutely devastated with grief and had let his property go downhill. So all of the locals planned to go round to his farm, mend some of the neglected fences and reap one of his fields to feed the cattle. The women would supply the food for the men, do some bits and pieces in the house and tidy up the place in general. I found it particularly fascinating that fine, sunny day, when all the neighbours headed for the farm to help out.

Every lane and every thoroughfare en route to the farm were jam-packed with locals carrying their tools and their food. Over fifty years later, that very same picture came to mind while I was watching that excellent movie *Witness*, starring Harrison Ford. Only that time, the people who all descended on the farm to help build a new barn were the lovely Amish people – the ladies in their old-fashioned clothes and the men with long beards. Incidentally, the Amish are a US Mennonite sect which traces its origins back to Jakob Amman, a seventeenth-century Mennonite bishop. The dictionary tells me that they are 'a Protestant sect that rejects infant baptism, church organisation and the doctrine of transubstantiation and in most cases refuses military service'. Okay, so I am digressing, but I like to learn and I find facts like that very interesting!

Anyway, my job was to lug all the boxes of pies and pasties around to the farm. But it was one of my most enjoyable days since I was parted from my big sister. The Witch buggered off somewhere while I mingled with all the other people on the grass outside the house. It was a lovely day, everybody was in a happy mood – especially old Uncle Sid who was knocking back the cider as if there was no tomorrow. And, like a starving animal, I had eaten so many of the Cornish pasties I thought I might throw up. Then came the shout from one of the beefy, Cornish farmers. 'We be a-going down to the bottom field to cut it. Bring all the food and drink and the guns down there, okay?' So everyone picked up their stuff and followed the tractor and the reaper down to the bottom field. I settled myself down over by the far hedge as they started cutting the grass. Suddenly, all hell broke loose. As the grass was being cut, so the rabbits and the field mice made a run for safety under a barrage from the shotguns. How one of the kids, or even one of the onlookers, didn't get shot, I'll never know. The guys firing the shotguns were not only wild, they were also all well boozed-up on cider. Surprisingly, nobody got injured and, even more surprisingly, there were plenty of dead rabbits to share among the locals. Believe me, if you haven't had the pleasure of eating meat for quite a while, then rabbit stew tastes like the finest feast! It's a strange fact, but we humans always seem to just remember the good things in life and conveniently forget the bad!

Conversely, my chilblains were weeping and getting even more painful and my bad nightmares and my bed-wetting were getting worse. These obvious signs of a young lad in distress were aggravated even more by longer spells in the woodshed for what the Witch decreed as 'wilful disobedience of a proper adult'. I must have looked and smelt a bit of a wreck, because even my schoolteacher, who generally never took a blind bit of notice of me or of any of the other vacs, said one day: 'What be the matter with your fingers lad and what be that funny smell about you?'

*Alfie's sisters Joan and Irene at school. (Joan Westmore's collection)*

'I got chilblains, sir,' I replied, happy that someone had at least noticed my plight. 'And that funny smell,' I went on, bringing a chuckle from the class, 'is because that bleedin' Witch I live with keeps chucking me in the freezing cold bleedin' woodshed and I keep peeing the bed.' He stepped back and his nostrils dilated as he caught a whiff of me. Then, just the slightest look of concern crossed his face as he said. 'Watch your language boy, go back to your seat and I'll look into it.' To give him his due, he must have had a quiet word in the Witch's ear, because things were never quite as bad again. Suddenly, I was sitting at the dinner table on a regular basis – even when the lady in the green uniform wasn't due to make her sporadic visits. I wouldn't say the Witch was exactly motherly towards me – she wasn't the slightest bit worried about my welfare. Her only concern was keeping the money coming in!

Suddenly, one bright sunny day – it must have been the start of summer – my Mum appeared on the doorstep with my two sisters and my dreadful ordeal was over. I was off like a shot, running down the lane and screaming out like a mad person – without as much as a goodbye or a backward glance! I left it to my Mum and my sisters to collect all of my belongings while I made a bee-line for the bus stop! After that terrible experience I could well have been scarred for life and grown up a nutcase, or even a psychopath. But, luckily, apart from monstrous nightmares well into adulthood, I became a kindly person without a hint of a bad temper and with a strong sense of humour. I've always taught myself a message in life, and it works for me. If you're at rock bottom and you're at the end of your tether – maybe with the loss of a loved one, or severe domestic traumas – remember this: the only way left for you is upwards!

## ALL TOGETHER AGAIN IN PERRANPORTH

I well remember that our eventual arrival in Perranporth was a time of great joy and happiness for me. At long last I was free from my tormentor. No more clumps round the ears, no more pain and abuse and no more humiliation, bed-wetting and dark woodsheds. With the benefit of hindsight, I could well have been one of the luckier evacuees in Cornwall. I only had to suffer the mental and physical abuse for one winter. What about the unknown number of other poor kids who were cursed with their tormentors, year after year? I remember, fifty years later when I was a London cabbie, and one of the other guys in the café was relating his evacuee experiences. He and his two brothers were evacuated to a farm deep in the country. To cut a long story short, they were almost starved by the brute of a farmer and his boozy wife who were always down the village pub. So, one dark night they decided to run away and make their way back to the East End of London. I don't know how in God's name they managed it, but they eventually hitchhiked all the way back home. Their close-knit East End family were absolutely appalled when they saw the state the kids were in, so they decided to do something about it. Their father and his three brothers were all London cabbies, so one day soon after, they piled into one of their taxis and headed for this particular farm, with two of the wives also in tow. Imagine the surprise of the brutish farmer when they arrived? Suffice to say they beat the shit out of him before dumping him into the muddy pig sty! The boozy farmer's wife was given the 'treatment' by the two angry wives as well!

My arrival in Perranporth had coincided with our country's lowest ebb in the Second World War. My keen young ears had perked up on grown-ups saying things like 'Jerry's big push has put our lads in trouble at Dunkirk' and 'it won't be long before Adolf comes across the Channel and lands on our island.' The faces were very serious, but I didn't really have an inkling of what they were talking about. Perranporth was a pretty little Cornish seaside town. We were staying with other evacuee families in a hotel way up on the top of the hill overlooking the town. I can always remember the steps opposite our hotel that led steeply down to a beach that seemed to stretch for miles.

It was only much later that I discovered this huge stretch of golden sands had been a popular venue for motorcycle races before the war. Now, the whole length of this lovely beach looked like a veritable scrapyard, with mile after mile of rusty barbed wire and equally rusty scaffolding. I was informed by one of the bigger boys that these miles of scaffolding were tank-traps and they were to 'Stop Jerry invading England'. They failed miserably to stop a crowd of young lads climbing all over them and I hesitated to think of the outcome if a full battalion of well-armed German soldiers had ever arrived! What I saw of the old boys in the local Home Guard drilling with broomsticks instead of rifles didn't exactly instill confidence in any future encounter with the enemy!

Yet life was good for me in Perranporth. I had my Mum and my two sisters with me and even my little brother. Every day seemed to be sunny, that's probably because it was summer, and I used to spend hours on the beach with my mates. One of our favourite and more dangerous games was to sit on the bottom of the huge steps that led down to the beach as the tide came in. It was the age-old game of 'dare' that young boys like to play to prove their manhood. Believe me, when the tide raced in over those sands, it was scary and violent. But us young lads used to hang on to the iron rail for dear life in an effort to win the game. The first one to move up the steps to safety was 'chicken', while the rest of us just got soaked to the skin. How one of us wasn't swept away to a watery death, I'll never know. Strange to relate, but there never seemed to be any going to school or adults looking over us, but we survived.

One fine day, while we were playing on the sands, we noticed a group of men and a policeman gathered around a bundle on the beach. Being kids, we crept up to see what was going on and to find out why the copper was there. One of the locals was talking to the copper in a serious tone. 'Yarp officer,' he said in a strong Cornish accent, 'I be a-walking my dog and I did see him when the tide went out.' 'It be a crying shame,' replied the copper, 'by the look of his uniform he be one of our Merchant Navy boys. I expect a Jerry submarine got his ship out at sea and the tide has just washed him ashore.' The other grown-ups in the group just nodded their heads sadly and continued to look down at the bundle on the beach. This was too much for an inquisitive little urchin from London. I pushed past the grown-ups to have a good look at a real dead sailor. But I only saw some bare feet with the rest of the corpse covered in some sacking, before someone tugged at my hair and shouted angrily in a loud Cornish voice.

'Bugger off, this b'ain't be a bloody peepshow.' So, we all ran off down the beach laughing like stupid idiots and feeling just a little bit scared at what we'd witnessed.

I really enjoyed living in the hotel in Perranporth. The other families were all Londoners, many of them from the East End, and they all shared what they had and we all mucked in together. All of us lads had a whale of a time. It was as though I was on a permanent summer holiday. We were on the beach every day, swimming, catching crabs and playing football – this really was the seaside! Then suddenly, one fine day, our Mum said to us out of the blue: 'You kids, get all your things packed. The warden has just told me that we're being transferred to Newquay and we are going to have our very own place to stay.' Once again it was tears and trauma for me. I liked it where we were and I didn't want to move to Newquay. 'Can I stay here with my mates, Mum?' I said innocently, 'and you can come back for me when you leave Newquay?' My Mum had half a smile on her face listening to my childish remarks. Then she promptly cuffed me around the ear and told me to get my bag packed. So, once again I was on the move. I didn't have an inkling where Newquay was, it could have been anywhere for all I knew. But at least we were all together and we were going to have a real place of our own. For sure I liked Perranporth, but I was quite excited at the prospect of yet another adventure!

# FOUR

# NEWQUAY FOR THE DURATION

T he short train journey from Perranporth to Newquay stays in my memory because of what I, in my childlike innocence, perceived as a vision of row after row of white mountains en route to Newquay. I later discovered they were in fact old chalk pits. The train chugged slowly over a rickety old viaduct and finally came to a halt. This was the end of the line for the train, my family and me, this was Newquay. An equally rickety old grey bus took us through the town centre and dropped us off on the corner of a road that led towards the harbour. Stanley Cottages, a little row of charming white cottages at the top of the steep hill that led down to the harbour, was going to be our very own place for I didn't know how long.

It's very difficult to pinpoint the exact year of the war when we arrived. But again, with the benefit of hindsight, certain very special happenings always stay in your mind. I recall coming back from a trip to the harbour with my friends and seeing my Mum clutching a telegram to her chest and sobbing bitterly. Her eldest brother Alf – the uncle I had been named after – had been killed in the desert campaign against Rommel. So it must have been around 1942. I tried to console our Mum, but in all honesty I didn't really begin to comprehend the reason for her crying. How on earth can a kid of six or seven possibly relate to the horrors and suffering of war? Strange to relate, it must have been over fifteen years later when I decided to get married and we needed my Mum and Dad's wedding certificate that the real truth about my uncles and aunts finally surfaced. My Mum's maiden name was completely different from that of my Nan and Grandad and all of my aunts and uncles. It appears that my old Nan had had a liaison with another man before – or who knows, even after – she had married my Grandad, and my Mum was the result of that liaison. My old Mum had carried the shame of her illegitimacy secretly, right through to my manhood. And even then there had been an amateur attempt to erase the existing name on her wedding certificate. I never let on that I had discovered her secret up to the day that she died. It's also rather strange that my lovely wife discovered a similar secret four years after her mother had died and over twenty years after we were married.

Our short stay at Stanley Cottages was a good time for me. I had been enrolled in a local school that I recall was opposite Towan Beach and was an old, brown stone Wesleyan Chapel. I well remember my very first day when one of the teachers sent me out to the school garden with some of the other lads, put a hoe in my hand and said in a broad Cornish accent: 'Alright me lad, you'me get yourself busy with this 'ere 'oe.' What did I know about hoes? I was a city boy and I'd never ever seen one before and he didn't think to tell me how to use the damn thing! I didn't even know why I was yanked in by another teacher, given a clump round the ear and reported to the headmaster for destroying most of the lettuces and cabbages. Only later did I discover that a hoe is for weeding and not for chopping off the heads of vegetables!

I did learn one good thing during my stay at Stanley Cottages – I learned to swim like a fish. Well to be precise, I was thrown off the harbour wall by some of the bigger Cornish boys, simply because I was a vac and I had to learn to swim or I would have drowned. That's life or death! I've got a memory like an elephant. I never, EVER forget when someone has taken a liberty with me. Looking out of the windows of Stanley Cottages one day I noticed these big Cornish lads who had thrown me off the harbour wall going past on their bikes. Right, I thought, I reckon they are heading for the old café on the harbour wall to chat up the young waitresses.

It was payback time. I was spot on with my reckoning and, after following them down the hill, I saw their bikes parked at the side of the old café. I had a quick peep in the window and made sure they were busy at the counter with their backs to me. Don't be too greedy, I thought to myself, just a couple of bikes will suffice in the high tide. So I picked up the first bike and after much huffing and puffing, I managed to toss it over the harbour wall and dashed back to dump the second one into its watery grave. Even that still didn't satisfy me – my revenge wasn't complete. I needed to see their faces when they came out of the café and found themselves two bikes short. I made a bee-line for the trees and bushes at the land end of the harbour wall and waited in eager anticipation. Revenge is sweet. The looks of utter bewilderment on their faces when they couldn't find the two bikes was well worth being tossed off the harbour wall not knowing how to swim! They were too thick to look over the harbour wall into the sea, not that they would have spotted the two bikes, long since sunk beneath the waves!

I recall a few weeks later seeing the same Cornish gang by the old harbour café and I couldn't resist giving them some stick. 'I 'ear someone nicked a couple of your bikes,' I said. The biggest bloke who was so ugly his face looked like an advert for keeping death off the road, snapped at me: 'Some effing bugger nicked them and threw them into the sea and when we find that bugger we're going to do him up good and proper.' I didn't want to push my luck, so I just walked past them saying caringly and innocently. 'What a crying shame, who would want to do a terrible thing like that?' Incidentally, when this book is eventually published and one of those big Cornish lads – now well into his seventies – just happens to read this particular story, I would like to offer my apologies for being a really rotten kid. But hey, as Del Boy in *Only Fools and Horses* is fond of saying: 'He who dares, wins!'

Me and my mates seemed to be on the beach every day. I can't honestly remember if it was during the long summer vacations but I have a sneaking feeling that we played truant most of the time. In fact, I know full well we

*Young Alfie at about twelve years of age. (Author's collection)*

bunked off school, because I was the ringleader. It just had to be me who told all the lies to teachers and parents alike, not that any of the teachers gave a tinker's cuss about some absent vacs. As for my old Mum, she was on another planet of deep grief and didn't come back into the real world for many weeks.

Our little gang, all strong swimmers by now, had this game of chicken that still brings a shudder of fear to me even to this day. The harbour wall facing Towan Beach had a large drainage tunnel bored through it to stop the harbour flooding. So when there was a high tide, the water used to rush through this tunnel at a frightening speed and spill into the sea. But there was a danger, a big danger. The tunnel exit by the beach had a tight wire mesh across the whole face, so at high tide the tunnel could easily become a watery grave for anybody trapped inside. But, would you 'Adam and Eve it' – all our gang used to sit in this tunnel in our swimwear, nervously waiting for the water to rise. The first to swim out was chicken. I liked to think of myself as a Jack the Lad and leader of the pack, and quite often I never left the tunnel until the sea had almost reached the roof! If my ol' man had seen my stupidity, I would have got a real good belting! Another one of our hair-raising pastimes was to shin up the sheer grass-covered cliff at the rear of the harbour like mountain goats to pick crab apples. I often wondered why we bothered with our tiring and dangerous climb, because they were sour and inedible and we always finished up throwing them at each other! There were never ever any adults looking after us. No wonder in later life I tended to be an over-protective father with my three kids!

These were wonderful balmy days for me. It was great living in Stanley Cottages. I enjoyed going down to the harbour and studying the gnarled old fishermen in their black, polo-necked jerseys and yellow waterproof trousers. I just sat there quietly looking at their weather-beaten faces as they puffed away on their old clay pipes and mending their nets. After a while, I got very chatty with some of them and sometimes they used to take me out on the boats for a short trip. Unfortunately, I was a city boy and not much of a sailor, spending most of my time leaning over the side being violently sick! I especially enjoyed the mackerel season, when all the fishing boats unloaded box after box of those beautiful, silver-coloured, shiny fish. Sometimes a shoal of mackerel would come into the harbour and appeared to commit suicide by getting themselves grounded in the shallow water. All my gang were in the shallows, diving around like madmen and trying to throw them onto dry land. It was fish aplenty in those far-off days and the fishermen all got a good very living. I often wonder if there are any fishing boats still left in Newquay – or in any other of the harbours in the South-West?

Then for some unknown reason, a big, strong healthy lad like me suddenly became very unwell and quite sickly. I started suffering from severe colds and painful sore throats, so I was dragged down to the local doctor's to get checked out. The short visit to the 'quacks' – that's what my parents called all doctors – still stands out in my memory, even after all these years. Incidentally, looking up the origin of the slang word 'quacks', I discovered that it originated during the terrible Bubonic Plague in London in 1664 – better known as the Black Death. Back then the famous medical experts of the day didn't have a clue about what caused the plague. Various theories were mooted – the most popular being that it was carried in 'bad air'. During the Plague, all the people who had the unenviable task of removing the hundreds of dead bodies from the streets wore strange-shaped masks to ward off any infections. These masks made them all look like ducks, hence the cockney slang for doctors – quacks.

After waiting some time, we were eventually shown into the doctor's surgery. I can distinctly recall a frosted-glass screen and the sound of liquid being poured from the other side, then stirred. The old doctor, with a shock of white hair, suddenly appeared from behind the glass screen and after some polite introductions, proceeded to look down my throat with a small torch. I tell you what, his breath positively stank of booze, whisky I reckon, with a mixer! He must have been swigging it behind the screen and it was still only early in the morning! Then he went into a huddle with my old Mum and I couldn't really hear what he was saying, but I wasn't all that bothered. He was in fact telling my old Mum that I had severe tonsillitis and required an immediate tonsillectomy to cure my problem. In those days it was the recognised practice to clip the tonsils in severe cases of tonsillitis. Not so today, the job can be done quickly with penicillin, or some other powerful drug, and no long-winded operation.

I didn't suspect anything when Mum asked me if I'd like to go to Truro with her on the train. In fact, I was highly delighted to go on a train again. I still didn't suspect anything when we arrived at the hospital. I really screamed the place down when I was whisked up to a ward and a couple of large nurses with big fleshy arms started taking off my clothes and telling me I was going to have a bath. Funny that, there was no sign of my old Mum, she'd done a runner yet again! I quietened down a bit when the two big nurses explained that I was just going to have just a little operation to make my throat better. But I was young and very, very modest. No way would I let those two big nurses see me with no clothes on, not realising they had seen a lot more than I could possibly show (and nothing has changed much ladies!). I made a right pest of myself on the ward for a few days until suddenly I was put on a trolley and wheeled down a long corridor to the operating theatre. I remember a bloke in a white gown and a mask coming towards me and pressing a pad over my nose. This was my first and last smell of chloroform, the evil-smelling drug that was used as an early anaesthetic. The following hour or so seemed like an absolute nightmare and remains clear in my memory. I was very groggy but still conscious. I felt somebody clamping my arms and legs down and there was this geezer in a white gown sticking something down my throat and making me feel sick and wanting to retch. I really did crash out then and the next thing I remembered was waking up in my bed with a sore throat and lots of blood on my pillow. A few days later, Mum came and picked me up and I was back home, safe and sound in Stanley Cottages. The operation worked for me and, touch wood, it has worked for over sixty years, even after puffing my pipe for four decades!

Then, like a bolt out of the blue, our Mum told us to pack up all our things because we were on the move again. Our destination this time around was the Pentire Hotel, just out of town by a local beauty spot called Fistral Bay. We would all still be together, but again we were sharing with other evacuee families. So, off I went once more on my Cornish travels!

FIVE

# ANOTHER MOVE
# TO PENTIRE

Our move to Pentire Head was almost like moving to another town.
Pentire is situated to the south-west of Newquay and consisted of
a headland jutting out into the Atlantic, with Fistral Beach on
one side and the River Gannel on the other. In those days there were only
a handful of tatty old houses on the headland, plus a few holiday cottages
scattered across the rocky and bleak shrubland. I probably wouldn't
recognise the old place if I visited it today. I do know that Fistral Bay is
now a Mecca for surfers from all over the world and, I would assume,
that an awful lot of redevelopment has taken place to accommodate the
thousands of tourists that flock to Newquay every summer. So, if you've
holidayed in the area over the past sixty-odd years, you'll have to excuse
me if I keep mentioning 'fields' or 'little lanes' that probably no longer
exist!

After leaving the town centre by going up the hill, I think it's called
Crantock Hill, then passing the golf links, you arrive at Pentire. To the
right of the headland was Fistral Bay, a lovely beach with miles of sand
dunes. To the left and down what used to be a lane, you come to the
Gannel. This is a small, tidal river that runs into the sea. Great fun to
play on the sands when the tide is out; fearsome and treacherous when
the high tides came rushing in, smashing itself against the rocky sides and
covering the river bed within a few minutes. Many's the time I misjudged
the tide and got caught on the wrong side and had to walk about 3 miles
home instead of 300 yards. It's well worth crossing the Gannel at low tide
and paying a visit to the very picturesque Crantock Village. Back in the
1940s, there used to be an old ship moored on the far bank that had been
converted into a maritime museum. I expect it's long gone by now.

Once more we were uprooted and waiting for the funny old bus that
would take us to yet another stopping place. Up the hill we went, heading
out of town. Left and right past the golf links, finally alighting at the

41

bus stop outside the Fistral Bay Hotel. We turned left after passing a big field with some horses, then struggled up a stony path to the Pentire Hotel. We were greeted at the door by a big buxom lady wearing a white pinafore. She introduced herself as 'Matron' and started a conversation with our Mum. As usual, I was too busy looking around to take much notice of what she was saying, but I did pick up on some of the snippets in her strong Cornish accent. 'This be how it works here,' said Matron, 'all the families be a-sharing,' she went on. 'That be the meat rations and the clothing coupons, they all be shared among everybody.' My dear old placid Mum, God bless her, who suffered years of physical abuse from a drunken bully of a husband; just stood there meekly nodding her head and repeating. 'Yus Missus, I understand wot you're a-saying.' I wasn't in the least bit interested about boring clothing coupons and meat rations, little realising that the meat rations were keeping me alive and healthy. I liked the look of the place and I needed to do some major exploring.

I soon teamed up with some new mates from London at the hotel and we spent many weeks playing on the sand dunes. Then we turned our hand to beachcombing on Fistral Bay. Again, I can't honestly ever remember going to school, certainly not on a regular basis. After a short period of time we turned out to be quite proficient beachcombers. We knew the bay, we got to know the tides and we always knew where the sea would wash up its best 'treasures'. Apart from a proliferation of ship's ropes – evil smelling with a mixture of tar and salt – plus the normal flotsam and jetsam you would find after a high tide. We managed to salvage and take back to the matron many useful items for the household, like large tin plates and saucepans and even a couple of kettles, plus many thick blankets, albeit wet, filthy, salty and smelling of the sea. Our matron knew her stuff, however, and she was excellent at improvising. Once the stinking blankets had had the boiling water and the soap suds treatment, plus a large dollop of Dettol, they were as good as new and helped to keep us warm through the long cold winter.

I suppose my best find and the one that made me very popular among the families, was the lard. I spotted it first as me and my mate were walking along the shore. It must have been about 3ft square and still wrapped in the greaseproof paper you used to see in the old grocery shops. It was just sitting there in the ebb tide moving ever-so gently, almost as though the tide was trying to take it back out to sea again. 'Come and 'ave a dekko at this,' I shouted to my mate. 'What is it, Alfie?' he said, running over and peering down rather nervously. 'What is it Alfie?' I replied, mimicking his timid voice. 'What the bloomin' 'ell do ya think it is, it's like gold dust to us, 'cos it's lard innit?' 'What's lard, Alfie?' said my mate, still looking down at the object as if it was about to explode. 'Oh for

Gawd's sake', I snapped. 'It'll be bloomin' dark soon and we'll get a right rollicking if we're late for our grub. If you ain't ever 'ad a slice of bread and dripping, then I ain't bovvering to explain.' I looked across at all the timber that had been washed ashore on the beach and, carefully weighing up our options. I said to him loudly, 'Make yourself bloomin' useful and sort out a couple of planks about 5ft long and bring 'em over 'ere.' 'What you gonna do, Alfie?' he said, after handing me the sea-soaked planks. 'Just lift the lard on to the planks when I tell you to and stop asking dopey questions, or we'll never get back before it gets bloomin' dark.'

I reckon we struggled for half a mile carrying that huge lump of lard on two planks back to the hotel. It looked like we were going to get a right telling-off at first, because it was getting dark and we were well late for our grub. But, as soon as the big matron saw the lard, she went all moony-eyed and ga-ga. She grabbed hold of me and gave me a big squeeze into

*A party for the Vacs.*
*(London Metropolitan*
*Archives)*

her ample bosom that smelled strongly of carbolic. 'Who'me be a clever boy then?' she chortled. 'Best be off to the kitchen and get out them big pots to boil it up,' she said, still hugging me furiously. The next day, every family in the hotel had a rare treat, a huge bowl of delicious dripping and I was flavour of the month for many days!

The modern, well-fed kids of today who lack for nothing, may find the significance of that story very difficult to comprehend. But us kids in the war had no fats whatsoever, be it butter, margarine or lard. Our staple diet consisted mainly of bread, potatoes and an assortment of vegetables, very rarely accompanied by a tiny piece of meat thrown into the pot in an effort to add some flavour and make it a casserole. What we need to remember is that Britain imported most of her food during the war and Hitler's U-Boats were sinking many of our ships. And if our boffins hadn't come up with the brilliant sonar detection device, we may well have all starved! With the benefit of hindsight, our total lack of fats and sugar as kids could well have proved a blessing in disguise. The latest scientific research indicates that adult health is almost certainly linked to what we eat as kids. Now, some researchers are saying that many of the children who grew up in the austere war years are among the healthiest adults and should enjoy longevity. It's a funny old world isn't it, childhood deprivation of food equals very healthy OAPs!

One of my favourite pastimes during my stay at Pentire was to go down to the Gannel when the tide was out, armed with my bamboo cane with a meat skewer tied to the end, and wade through the fast flowing stream, trying to spear flatfish, just like the Indians did in the films. My endeavours hardly ever brought any success. The only thing I can remember spearing was one of my feet! But, it was a wonderful way to enjoy a warm summer's day in the peace and quiet of the country. Other times I would wander off completely on my own to the far end of Pentire Head. Then I'd clamber down the rocks dangerously close to the huge waves breaking on the headland. I'd select a huge boulder that was farthest out to sea and just sit on it for hours, paddling my feet in the water and staring out at the ocean. I'd think of my Mum and my Dad and my brother and two sisters. And I'd think of London and the Blitz and sleeping down the Tube and the damp Anderson shelter. Then, I'd worry about whether my Nan and my aunties and uncles were still alive, or if any of my mates had been killed by the bombs. In fact, I would go over my young life in detail, trying very hard to rid my mind of the dreaded 'red monster' and of the terrible months I had suffered at the hands of the Witch. I suppose, looking back, you could say it was very helpful therapy of the mind. And I still do it when I'm playing my beloved golf to help to relax me.

The scary thing I often think about now was that not a living soul knew where I had gone. If I had slipped and got washed out to sea nobody would have known my fate. But it's only when you are mature that you start to worry. Young kids, especially young lads like me, never had any reason to feel fearful about climbing over slippery rocks on a stormy headland, simply because we could never perceive any dangers in our folly!

The sun always seemed to shine while I was living in the Pentire Hotel. I roamed the beaches and the golf links like a free spirit. So, apart from the distinct possibility of getting drowned or breaking my neck climbing cliffs, I was quite contented doing my thing.

It was every young boy's dream come true – I woke up one sunny morning, opened the curtains of my bedroom window that overlooked the L-shaped lane around the hotel and got the shock of my young life. There in front of me, and as far away as the eye could see, were lines of massive tanks, great big guns on wheels, trucks and jeeps and a whole army of soldiers in uniform, all wearing strange helmets. I flew down the stairs and crashed into the bosom of matron. 'Hold back there, young Alfie,' she said, putting a firm restraining hand on my shoulder. 'What be the big hurry?' 'I've just looked out of my bedroom window, Matron.' I gasped, 'and I fink the bloomin' Jerries have landed.' She let out a loud chuckle and ruffling my hair with her hand, she said: 'You'me got a real vivid imagination, young Alfie. Them b'ain't be Germans, them be Yanks and they be on our side in this terrible war.' I'd never heard of Yanks and I had no inkling where they came from, but I couldn't wait to go outside and greet them. From that very day, I've always reckoned the Americans to be the kindest and friendliest people I'd ever met. Can you possibly imagine the scene on that day? There was me, a scruffy young cockney, wandering among these huge soldiers who were all talking with a funny accent and puffing away on cigarettes and cigars. There were lots of officers around, all looking resplendent in their tailored uniforms. One of the officers must have been the boss-man because he had big, gold-leaf clusters on his shoulders and was surrounded by other officers who kept saluting him. Suddenly, he saw me and said in a loud and imposing voice: 'Looks like one of the locals have come to greet us guys.' The other officers standing next to him all turned around to look at me and started laughing – rather too heartily. You know the sort of laugh you have to make when your teacher cracks a joke that's not funny! 'Don't you call me a local mate,' I replied angrily, 'I come from London and I didn't ask to come 'ere.' 'Hey, hold your horses tiger,' said the bloke with the gold-leaf clusters, whacking his shiny stick against the side of his leg. 'We came over to fight the Krauts, not to mess with you London guys.' He sauntered off, closely followed by his entourage of junior officers who were all sniggering and looking back at me like a bunch of school kids.

I suppose my biggest initial surprise was to see all the black soldiers. As I stated earlier, back in London it was very rare to see one black man, let alone a whole company or more! Even at my tender age, I was growing up brainwashed by my bigoted Dad into believing that black people were different, or even inferior to us whites. Sadly, that bigotry was passed from generation to generation. That also showed among some of the young GIs as I got to know them. I loved the guys from the Deep South with their Southern drawl. They were so friendly and polite and always addressed me as 'Suh'. But as soon as a black GI walked past, they would shout out cruel things like: 'Where you going boy, you best go and pick that cotton'. Then they'd all sit around laughing and joking. Most of the black GIs just bent their heads and moved on without replying. But, I learned much later many of them joined the Military Police or SPs as the Yanks called them. With their prominent white helmets they were nicknamed 'Snowdrops' and were feared by the GIs. Anytime there was a brawl in a pub or a club involving American troops, the 'Snowies' would appear and start wading in with their batons. I suppose this could have been an outlet for their bitter resentment of being considered second-class citizens in their own country.

Meeting these black soldiers had quite a profound effect on me in later life and by the time I had become politically aware at the end of the 1950s, I followed the Civil Rights Movement with great interest and sympathy. Their imposing leader, Martin Luther King, was a truly great orator and his passionate speeches used to send shivers down my spine. On a personal level I thought, why should my hero, the great singer and world star Nat King Cole, have to stay in a 'coloureds only' hotel when he toured the American South? And why didn't the black people of America ever have equal civil rights to their white neighbours? Their sons, brothers and husbands were willing to fight and give up their lives for their country in both world wars. Surely that made them Americans to the core and equal citizens?

Nearly all the Yanks were very friendly. They missed their own kids and took a shine to me, this chirpy little cockney sparrow. Within a couple of days, the regular sentry patrols had a nickname for me, 'The Little Limey'. It wasn't until many years later that I discovered the derivation of the word 'Limey'. Way back in the days of the sailing ships and probably during the American War of Independence, many, many sailors met painful deaths due to scurvy. Then somebody discovered that eating lemons cured the terrible disease by providing vital Vitamin C. Not so the Brits. Whether by design or for reasons of economy, we decided to give our sailors limes.

Hence the Yanks' slightly derogatory term for the Brits, passed down through the generations!

I was a born scrounger and a cadger. If you didn't have the chat, then sometimes you didn't eat. My scrounging skills resulted in building up a nice little supply of chocolate bars plus dozens of sticks of chewing gum. I can't profess to be the very first person to have coined that well-known wartime saying to the Yanks – 'Got any gum chum?' – but it was certainly in my repertoire long before it was made famous by the comedians!

When I eventually went back to school after God knows how long, my supply of goodies became a valuable swapping commodity among my classmates. Bars of chocolate, Hershey Bars, I think they were called, never to be seen in sweetshops during the war, were like bars of gold. You could literally ask for the shirt off someone's back in exchange. The local adults were getting quite friendly towards me as well, simply because I also had a supply of Lucky Strikes, Camel and Chesterfield cigarettes. The Yanks used to give me packs because they wanted to hear me say. 'My Mum's dying for a fag.' Then they'd all fall about laughing like mad. How was I to know that in American terminology, a 'fag' had a different connotation?

The American troops were billeted in many of the big hotels in Newquay and we were forever hanging around the kitchens hoping to cadge or nick something. I can still remember the huge columns of wooden boxes stacked outside, with Coca Cola written on them. We used to take out one of the funny-shaped, empty Coca Cola bottles and hold them up to the sun so that light reflected through the thick glass like a prism. At other times we would peek into the communal shower rooms, specially constructed for the Yanks. What you have to remember is nobody but nobody, ever took a shower in the 1940s. This was a real revelation for us to see all those naked young bodies covered in soap suds, especially the black guys. We would creep up to their mess hall and watch the GIs queuing up for their grub or 'chow' as they called it. Again, for kids who existed on bread and jam, it was a revelation to see so much different food dished out. They had fried eggs and baked beans and huge steaks and, would you believe, even thick slices of pineapple on their steaks. At the time we envied the Yanks because they had so much more than us. In fact, we had nothing! But we couldn't possibly comprehend that many of these lovely guys would never see their families or loved ones again in the terrible battles to come in Europe. We were simply jealous and very hungry kids!

The tanks, guns, trucks, jeeps and soldiers seemed to be a permanent view from my bedroom window. I used to wander up and down the convoy, chatting to all the guys as they lay under the tanks and trucks, getting themselves oily and dirty. When the whistle blew for 'chow', out would come the dice and all down the convoy there would be groups of guys playing 'craps' for money – quite often, big money. These incidents came to my mind and made me grin many years later when I was doing my National Service in the RAF. It was strictly against Queen's regulations to gamble and you could be put on a charge if you were caught, which of course I was. Yet the Yanks gambled all the time, often with senior NCOs and, in some cases, with officers joining in! I think the Queen's regulations have got it just about right, because many of the American boys lost their whole paychecks.

One day, I was talking to my friend 'Sarge' and trying to cadge some more candy off him. I honestly thought Sarge was his real name and 'Corp' was the real name of his buddy. What did I know about the different ranks in the army? Sarge was a real nice gentleman. He had told me he was a farmer from the Mid-West and that he had five kids. He must have been well over 6ft tall, with big shoulders and big hands. What absolutely fascinated me about him was that his chest hair always sticking out of the top of his green khaki tee-shirt. He had a tanned face with fine white teeth and when he spoke, it was like the sound of deep, rumbling thunder. His buddy, Corp, was totally the opposite. He was half Italian, small and wiry and his hometown was New York.

'I'm sorry, Little Limey,' drawled Sarge, 'no more candy because we'll be shipping out soon.' This was an absolute disaster. The Yanks had helped me and my family and many of the other families to survive, thanks to their generous gifts of tins of food. I grabbed his hand and led him to the front of the convoy, just under my bedroom window. 'See that lamp post, Sarge?' I said, pointing to an old-fashioned street lamp with big glass window panes at the top. 'Before you leave, can you please hide some candy bars in the long grass at the bottom. Please, please, Sarge,' I said, clutching his hand very tightly.

I stayed up late that night and slept like a log, I never heard a sound. The next morning I pulled open the bedroom curtains and all the Yanks and all the tanks and guns and trucks and jeeps had vanished, just like magic. This made me feel very sad because many of them had become my friends and they were lovely people. After breakfast, I walked outside to see if there were any of my mates still around in the lane, but they had all gone. The only signs they had ever been there were the tyre marks and the deep tracks made by the tanks. Suddenly I remembered the old lamp post and I put my hand down into the deep grass and found a package addressed to the 'Little Limey' from 'The Guys'. I was touched and more than sixty years on, I'm still very touched by this marvellous generous gesture. These brave young men were getting ready to join the largest armada the world had ever seen, in an attempt to invade Nazi-controlled Europe. Many would be killed and maimed in the bloody battles to come. Yet they had found the time – the very night they were pulling out – to have a 'candy collection' for a young cockney cadger. Isn't it any wonder that I have a deep and lasting affection for the American people? I can only hope and pray that my friends Sarge, Corp and all their buddies made it home safely again after the war. I was just a young kid of nine, so how did I know what these brave young men would have to face? I've often wondered in the ensuing years if any of my American buddies from Newquay were on Omaha or Utah Beach at the D-Day landings.

Life wasn't quite the same at Pentire after my American mates had departed. I still did the beachcombing and wandered down to the Gannel with my home-made spear. But I spent a great deal more of my time sitting alone on the rocks at the end of the headland and thinking what my American mates were doing. I honestly thought they had gone off for a training exercise and that they would return to Pentire at any moment. But they never came back to me and sadly, many of them never probably came back to their families and loved ones. I still like to think that their short friendship with the 'Little Limey' maybe helped them to think of home.

Then, one day, out of the blue, our Mum said we were on the move again. I said my goodbyes to all my mates and matron once again smothered my head in her ample bosom saying, with a twinkle in her eye. 'You'me be a good lad for your Mummy, Alfie, and if you're a bugger, I'll come over and smack your bum'. The Cornish are a funny people, they use 'bugger' for everything. Our final destination before the end of the war was the Cliff Close Hotel. It was situated at the other end of Newquay, just a stone's throw from the station. It was actually the first building on the right, past what I can only call a 'sunken lane'. I have since learned that this sunken lane used to be a tram-track before the war. So, we packed up all our bits and pieces, walked down to the main road and waited for the old bus. Yet again, we went past the golf course and down Crantock Hill and through the town. We all piled out at the bus-stop, just before the station, and eyed our new home from the outside. To me, it looked all right. It had probably been an average-priced sort of hotel before the war and had seen better days. It had a big, sloping terraced front garden and a huge back garden. We could have a good laugh here, I thought to myself, just as long as we are not sharing with any old miseries and a matron telling us what to do all the time. Luckily as it turned out, we had the whole place to ourselves!

I staggered up the steep stone steps of the overgrown, terraced garden, still dragging my battered old suitcase. I can still picture the big old front door – it reminded me of a church with a stained-glass window! Mum put the huge key into the lock and with a loud creak and a groan, the door swung open. Us kids dashed inside to explore and raced up the imposing staircase, throwing open all the different doors on the top landing. There were great squeals of delight as we counted all the bedrooms and all the bathrooms. It looked as though we could each have a bedroom and a bathroom all to ourselves! Then we dashed downstairs and into the massive garden around the back of our new home. This is great, I thought to myself. I could have a dog and a cat and any other animal I wanted!

# SIX

# OUR FINAL MOVE

This final move was akin to moving to another town. We had started off in the centre of Newquay by the harbour, then moved to the southernmost point. Now we were back on the northern edge. Everything was new to me – there were new beaches to discover, new cliffs to climb, an RAF aerodrome to check out and a boating pond behind the station by the old viaduct. There were still plenty of Yanks in town after the front-line troops had departed and the Great Western Hotel – just a stone's throw away from our hotel Cliff Close – housed the American officers. I think it was every Thursday evening that they had a motion-picture show in the big ballroom that looked out on to the garden. So, I would arrive in their hotel garden every Thursday evening, find a gap in the heavy curtains that had been drawn across the opened French windows and enjoy a free film! Bob Hope, Bing Crosby and Dorothy Lamour in all their famous 'Road' movies. I saw them all, long before they were released in Britain. I did this Thursday 'visit' for many weeks and not once did any of the American officers rumble me. They just sat there in the dark puffing away at their ciggies and enjoying the film. Whether they even saw me in the dark is another matter. With hindsight, I suppose they were lucky I wasn't a German spy with a suitcase full of grenades!

I remember once playing in the private gardens of the Great Western Hotel. God only knows how I got in there past the guards. Suddenly I tripped and fell on a great lump of jagged glass that pierced the flesh on the left side of my knee. I went down as if I had been pole-axed, screaming in agony, with blood splattering all over the place. The next thing I remembered was this wonderful smell in my nostrils. I looked up and saw a beautiful, blond-haired woman wearing an American officer's uniform, smiling down at me with the most perfect teeth I had ever seen. 'Let's have a look and see what you've done to yourself honey,' she said in soft, Southern drawl. 'Oh, that's not nice at all,' she said, wiping the gaping wound, 'I guess if you're a brave enough soldier, I can stitch it up.' I just lay there in absolute agony, looking up at this beautiful creature with the sweet smell and thinking, am I dead? Is she an angel? No way was I going to let this lovely lady think I was a coward, so I said in a wobbly, nervous voice 'Do what you have to do, missus, I ain't scared.' I often wish on reflection that I'd kept my big mouth shut and waited for an ambulance, because what followed was so painful, it made me feel sick. Two other lady officers held me down while my 'angel' proceeded to sew me up like an old pin cushion. No painkillers, no ether, no anaesthetic. Just a needle and thread on skin and bone, with me wailing like a banshee! They bound the wound and lifted me up, even though I was a bit groggy. 'Okay honey,' she said. 'You just scoot off back to your Ma and tell her you've been a very brave soldier.' With that she gave me a soft kiss on the cheek and the other two lady officers gave me a cuddle and pressed some Hershey Bars into my sweaty little hands. Then, they were gone and I never saw them again. Many years later, at the pictures with my mates, I often used to sit in the dark and fantasise that the lovely blonde lady on screen wasn't really Lauren Bacall, or even Betty Grable, but my American Cornish angel. Needless to say, when I arrived back home, nobody even noticed the bandage or my face. I was forever grazing myself and coming home wearing bandages and plasters. So what was new? If I can remember correctly, a couple of weeks later I pulled the stitches out myself!

On the subject of the Yanks still in town, I kept hearing people saying that the Yanks were: 'Overpaid, over-sexed and over here.' I didn't really understand what it meant, but my cunning cockney brain started to see the possibility of a good earner when they started whistling after my eldest sister. By this time, she must have been about sixteen and was blossoming into a shapely and attractive young lady. But she was always lumbered with me if she wanted to go out, because our Mum used to say: 'You stay with your bruvver, Joanie, and keep away from those bleedin' randy Yanks.' She certainly got plenty of wolf-whistles whenever we walked past them! They would shout out things like 'Hello honey, you gonna keep me warm tonight?' or, 'D'ya wanna be my pin-up baby?' Then she'd start chatting to them and shout across to me: 'Don't you dare tell Mum, Alfie, or I'll belt you one.'

This was the start of my little earner. As time passed, she got very friendly with some of the Yanks. They would ask her to go for a walk with them, with me following behind of course! I distinctly remember the Yanks always loved to walk her to this quiet, nearby orchard. Then the guys used to say to me. 'Here's some candy and some gum buddy. Just you sit here on the wall and we'll be back in a couple of minutes.' What did I know what was going on? I was getting goodies for just sitting on a wall for a few minutes and if they wanted to pick some apples, so what!

I was always up the front when the Yanks were talking, sitting outside their hotels and often picked up on some of their chat. I didn't have a clue who Ike, Uncle Joe or Monty were, but I joined in as though the names were familiar to me. Then they started talking about the likes of Truman and Dewey and about who was going to win the American election. 'Hey kiddo,' one of them said to me, with a big grin on his face. 'Who ya gonna put your money on for the presidential election, Dewey or that other bum Truman?' I didn't have a clue what he was talking about but it was all about ingratiating myself for future goodies. I'd never heard, or seen, the name Dewey before, but I did remember the other name above some of the pubs, Truman's Beers, or something like that? So, I tried to look as studious as possible before I finally answered. 'I fink Truman will be the winner by a short 'ead.' The Yanks started to fall about with hilarious laughter as though I had cracked a real funny joke. 'Hey you dumb Limey son of a bitch,' said one of them. 'Don't you know that Dewey is the red-hot favourite and we've all put our paychecks on his nose?' Now I had the dead needle because he'd called me by that rude name and I wasn't going to back down. 'You can put your money on his nose or up his arse for all I care,' I retorted angrily, amid screams of laughter from the other guys. 'But Dewey ain't gonna win, 'cos Truman is.' These guys had already shipped out before the news filtered through that Harry S. Truman had indeed become the new President of the United States. I often wonder if those guys ever told the funny story on the battlefields of Europe about that 'dumb Limey son of a bitch', who correctly picked the rank outsider in the presidential election? I like to think so.

By this time, I had a new love and a new mate. My new love was collecting birds' eggs with my new mate Donald Patience. I'll never forget old Don, we were really good mates for many months and almost inseparable. After the war, I was invited up to his house in Finsbury Park, not far from where I lived, for Sunday dinner. But our friendship didn't work out in London due to that dinner. I could never be real mates with someone whose mother was so posh that they had roast potatoes and boiled potatoes ALL on the same plate! It was so embarrassing for a yob like me! Don and I used to climb nearly every tree that had a nest and scour every cliff that had a bird population. I shudder when I think of what we got up to. The steepest cliffs in the area were called, appropriately enough, Baker's Folly. Would you believe that I used to climb down the sheer cliffs from the top, holding on to a tatty old rope held by Don? The seagulls and other birds, who were nesting on the cliff face, were screaming and dive-bombing me while I raided their nests. Probably more by luck than judgement I never fell or slipped. Then it was back to base with our haul of eggs, stick a pin in both ends and blow out what was inside. It took us a while to realise that we needed to collect the eggs early on in the year – well before the chicks started to form inside. Then somehow, or from somewhere, don't ask me where, I had managed to obtain a proper collector's box to exhibit the eggs. This was my pride and joy for many long months. Lovely polished, shiny wood and a real brass lock. Lots of little sections inside all lined in a brown fur to put different-sized eggs in. The eggs were all lovingly wrapped up in cotton wool – with a glass front for all my friends to see. I became quite an expert on the names of all the assorted eggs that we had managed to swipe!

When I finally left to return to London, I remember well my old Mum saying to me in no uncertain manner: 'Alfie, you ain't taking that bleedin' great box of eggs 'ome with you. Get shot of it.' I was heartbroken. That 'bleedin' great box' represented months of hard work and scratched knees, torn fingers and many happy memories. But Mum was the guv'nor and I had to do her bidding. If my memory serves me right, I believe I swapped my complete precious collection for an air pistol that was supposed to fire real lead pellets – it didn't work!

These were happy times for the family and me at Cliff Close. Again the sun always seemed to shine, I roamed the different beaches in the area from dawn 'til dusk and as for schooling, once again, I can't remember too much of that. One of the most popular pastimes for Don and me, was, again, a very dangerous thing to do. We would wait for the tide to go fully out, then race across the different beaches and clamber over the rocks heading north to the airfield at St Columb Minor – or was it St Columb Major? Then we'd climb up the cliff that led to the airfield and peer through the fence at the planes. I never remembered seeing any guards, certainly nobody ever challenged us. Our return trip back to where we started was always a bit hairy because the tide was on the turn and starting to come in quite quickly. We'd clamber over rocks giggling like mad when a mighty wave soaked us. Then we'd make a mad dash for it across the sand before another wave came in. We nearly always made it back to our starting point at Towan Beach. All except for one particular time when we misjudged the tide and were forced to scale a huge cliff to safety because the sea had cut us off. I arrived back home that evening very late and bleeding from grazed knees and soaked to the skin. There was certainly no sympathy or concerns from my family about what had happened to me. I just got a clump around the ear and told to go upstairs and clean myself up!

Our Dad started to appear at weekends on a regular basis. Mum told us that he was helping to build an airfield in the area. I recall showing my Dad some of my haunts on the beach and once or twice we would go swimming together. I can distinctly remember his funny-looking swimming trunks made in a strange, shiny red material, cut very high at the front and done up with a belt of white plastic. I thought they were hilarious. Unfortunately, I never really had much affinity with my old Dad. I think he was a boozer and a bit of a bully. He'd served in the Far East in the Duke of Cornwall's Light Infantry between the wars and still suffered terrible bouts of deep-seated malaria. Mixed with the regular booze, this could make him a very violent man. He was certainly the biggest bigot it has ever been my misfortune to meet in my lifetime. Every single black man he ever met he called 'Johnny', a derogatory term used in army slang. Quite often – especially when he'd had a drink – he would attempt to pass on his bigotry to me. 'Oh yes, boy,' he'd say. 'Your Johnnies ain't like us white people. Out in Egypt they live like bleedin' animals.' I recall his utter disgust when the *Empire Windrush* arrived in England in the early 1950s, full of families from the Caribbean. These people had forsaken their tropical paradise to answer the call for the lack of unskilled labour from Great Britain. Yet, bigots like my Dad, and there were plenty of them, held up their arms in total despair and said it was the end of England! Thankfully, they were proved wrong and we are now a thriving, multi-cultural nation.

My old Dad became a prison warder after leaving the army and actually served at the dreaded Pentonville Prison close to my Nan's house. The story goes that he got the sack for being involved in a scam to get money and various other goodies in to the cons. The villains on the outside used to catch and kill pigeons. Then they'd cut open the birds, scrape out their innards, put the 'gear' inside, then sew them up again. During the night they would toss the birds over the prison walls at the appropriate location. My Dad was accused of being involved by picking up the pigeons that contained the gear. He naïvely pleaded his innocence, saying he just picked up the dead birds because felt sorry for them. But they sacked him anyway, though they didn't nick him! If ever I upset him, which was often, off would come his big, thick leather belt and he'd whack me all round the room with it. But things change with the passing of time and parents need to understand that their kids can appear to become adults almost overnight! He tried his leather-belt bullying once too often when I was a strapping fifteen-year-old back in London. I grabbed his wrist as he took off his leather belt and said quietly: 'No more Dad, that's the finish of it, I'm not a kid anymore.' I saw the look in his eyes, his anger turned to embarrassment, then almost to sadness. The realisation suddenly dawned on him that the years had rolled by and I was reaching manhood. Strangely enough, I felt sorry for him, it was the end of an era.

Once again I got into trouble on one of my Dad's visits. I was too young to comprehend the significance of the creaking bed springs from my parents' room. And when I told my big sister what I'd heard and asked her innocently what it was all about, she clumped me around the ear and said she was telling Mum that I was being 'dirty'. It took me many years to work out why I'd got a clump around the ear!

As time went by, it was noticeable, even to a kid like me, that my parents and all our neighbours and the people in town were smiling a lot more. One fine summer's day, Don and I decided to walk into town via the cliff path and Towan Beach. Every postcard I've ever seen of Newquay depicts the island off Towan Beach. I learned recently the posh house on the island was owned by an ex-politician called Lord Long and that he was selling it. So, if ever they make this book into a film, I think I'll buy it! Anyway, as we walked across the spacious grass lawn that leads to the town, we couldn't help but notice the deep trenches that had been dug facing out to sea. They were obviously constructed to counter any Nazi invasion. However, a quick peek down into the trenches showed evidence, not of Germans, but of Yanks having been ultra-'friendly' with the young female population of Newquay!

Suddenly we heard the sound of a brass band so we made a bee-line towards the music. It was a real parade, marching through town with lots of people clapping and cheering. I loved the sound of the brass band and the tuba going 'oom-pah, oom-pah,oom-pah'. I had to chuckle when I saw all these blokes in funny outfits with little bells on their trousers, waving what looked like girls' scarves and dancing to the marching band. I thought they looked like a bunch of pansies. People were all laughing, clapping, skipping and hopping. We discovered later that this was an annual event called the Cornish Floral Dance, and it had been going on for many centuries. Don and me joined in the parade and started hopping to the sound of the band and waving our hankies about like the other pansies. It was all a big giggle but the whole atmosphere of people being happy, clearly indicated that the war was going our way. In fact, by then the Allies had already pushed on and liberated Paris.

It was a massive surprise to me, and a great disappointment, when my best mate Don told me that he was going back to London. I think Don was a bit older than me and much more studious and a bit posh. 'My Dad says Jerry's on the run,' he said to me one day. 'So it will be safe for us to go back to London.' 'Listen Don, you don't wanna go back to London,' I said, really believing I could dissuade him. 'I'll have a word with my Mum and you can stay with us.' He smiled at me, ruffled my hair in a matey fashion and said: 'You're a lad, Alfie. You're really quite dopey at times. How on earth can I stay with you and your Mum and leave my own family?' So, that was the end of a great friendship and the beginning of the end of my stay in Cornwall.

Things were never quite the same after Don left. For sure, I had lots of mates but none of them were like Don. We still roamed the beaches and the cliffs and we still got in trouble with the law for scrumping apples. In fact, I was fined £1 in the local magistrates court for scrumping and given a belting by my Dad. Some twenty years later, when I had to list my convictions to be accepted onto the Knowledge of London test, I inadvertently forgot this fine. Not so the Public Carriage, the ruling body of London's licensed taxi trade. The conviction was still on my file and I got a right rollicking for not declaring it!

The Yanks were still in town and my big sister's latest boyfriend was billeted in the hotel just across the lane from us. Every night she would stand swooning at her bedroom window while he played the same songs on his record player. One was called, 'Amour Amour, Amour', all soppy and lovey-dovey. The other one had a Latin American title that went on about 'If you go, if you leave me alone, each little kiss will be mine and my life will be gone, Bess-sam-e-mucho, kiss me my darling and tell me you'll always be mine'. Or something like that! The third record was a very popular comic tune at the time entitled or so I thought, 'Mairzy Dotes and Dozey Dotes'. For years I used to sing the song thinking the words were: 'Mairzy dotes and dozey dotes and little lambsy-divey, tittly-tattly too, wouldn't you?' It was only very recently my dear wife informed me that the words were actually: 'Mares eat oats and does eat oats and little lambs eat ivy, kids'll eat ivy too, wouldn't you?' I'm slow but I get there in the end!

I didn't go a lot on my sister's boyfriend when one fine day we just happened to bump into him by accident. I was still her minder, you'll notice. For sure, he was dark and handsome – as my sister had told me a million times. He looked the business in his smart uniform with the stripes on his arm. Mind you, every Yank I ever saw had at least one stripe on his arm. Did they get a stripe just for going to England? This guy, I think his name was Raef, looked for all the world like a Mexican bandit. He was positively swarthy and had grown this ridiculous moustache that drooped down either side of his pie-hole, making him appear almost mournful! He kept touching my sister and calling her 'Conchita'. No, I didn't rate him at all, and told my sister she could do better than a Mexican bandit!

All of my London mates seemed to be going back and one day, sure enough, our Mum announced with a beaming smile on her face. 'We've found a place to live in London, Alfie, and we're going 'ome next week.' I wasn't too pleased with this news because I now liked the life in Cornwall. I reckoned I was more Cornish than a Londoner and I didn't want to go back to that dirty old place 'Well,' I said to Mum, 'you can go back, but I ain't.' I got a clump around the ear for that remark and when she told my Dad at the weekend what I had said, he gave me a good hiding.

We packed our battered old suitcases for the last time and I went out into the garden and said a tearful goodbye to my two lovely dogs who were buried there. Patch was my companion and my bedmate for ages and when he died I never thought I could love another dog. Then I was given Sheba and I grew to love her even more. Now I had to leave them. I felt very sad. We'd had some great times, all of us playing out in the huge garden. One of our favourite games, I recall, was sliding down the big grass verge towards the lane that before the war used to be a tram-track. I well remember that day when this posh boy turned up and joined in our game. I had spoken to him once before on the beach and he'd told me that his father owned the jeweller's shop just up the road opposite the station. Anyway, after a while he picked up his parcel and said he'd have to go because he was delivering some stuff for his Dad. A while after he'd left I was chasing my dog around the garden and I came across this parcel by the grass verge. I picked it up and took it inside to show my Mum. My two sisters crowded round while Mum cut the string and opened the box. 'Oh my,' gasped Mum, as she looked into the box, 'I fink you've found the bleedin' crown jewels, Alfie'. My two sisters pushed forward to have a look into the box shoving me out of the way. 'Gor' blimey Mum', they chorused. 'We're gonna be rich.' 'Wot's going on?' I said, pushing myself to the front for a good look inside. I couldn't believe my eyes. The box was packed full of diamond rings, necklaces and gold bangles, just like a treasure chest in the old pirate films. My two sisters were jumping up and down and screaming out in great excitement. 'Let's flog it all and buy our own house in London.' But I had tumbled straight away who the 'treasure chest' really belonged to, so I said to them. 'Naw, you can't do that, we'll all get nicked. This belongs to the posh bloke who's just been playing with us. Anyway, I'd better take it back before his Dad calls out the coppers.' So, I walked up the road to the jeweller's shop clutching my precious parcel. And, would you believe all I got from the boy's father was a 'Thank you very much' and the threat to belt his son when he returned!

Needless to say, when my old Dad came back at the weekend, he went barmy after being told the story. 'You ain't got no savvy at all, have ya?' he snarled at me in a raging anger. 'We could have cashed in on your find and got ourselves out of this bleedin' dump.' He was muttering and swearing to himself and still he went on and on. 'All we had to say was we didn't find nuffing, then when there was a reward offered, we'd find it. But no, not you', he whined, 'forever the bloody Honest John and we finished up with sod all, didn't we?' I don't think my old Dad ever forgave me for doing what I thought was the natural thing to do. Even the poorest of kids are basically honest, until they're taught otherwise!

Now the time had come to leave. I trudged despondently away from the Cliff Close Hotel, dragging my battered old suitcase and followed my family up the road a couple of hundred yards to the station. I had roamed the countryside and the beaches as a free spirit for months. Now I was returning to a place that I didn't know and a place that evoked bad memories from my earliest childhood. No wonder I was feeling grumpy. I stared out of the window as the train pulled out of Newquay and chugged slowly over the viaduct. I could see the tennis courts and the boating lake below; I remembered all the great times I'd had there, especially on a cold winter's day with thick snow on the ground when Don and I had a great time on the tennis courts throwing snowballs. The train picked up speed, the white mountains flashed by in the blink of an eye and, suddenly, my childhood was behind me and I was heading for a new life in London and manhood. But, would I be happy and would smelly old London ever take the place of lovely, scenic Cornwall? We shall see.

# SEVEN

# RETURN TO WAR-TORN LONDON

Stepping off the train at Paddington station was a bit of a weird sensation for me. It felt like I was leaving a time capsule, that the four and a half years or so that I'd been away had never really happened. Could it all have been just a figment of my boyhood imagination?

*Back to war-torn Islington. (Islington Libraries)*

*Brecknock Road battered. (Islington Libraries)*

Nothing had changed much since that frightening day all that time ago, except for the rows of bomb-torn houses that I noticed as we steamed through West London. As we got nearer Central London, the bomb-damage got even worse and some areas looked like a flattened wasteland. On arrival, the station still echoed to the sound and smell of the locomotives blowing their steam boilers – there were still hundreds of people flocking around, most of them in uniform. I picked out the many brown belts of the army officers, the white-blancoed belts of the RAF boys and the sailors in their bell-bottom trousers. Only this time around it was different for me. I had returned as a big strapping lad of nearly ten years old with a healthy complexion after years spent in the country air. No longer were the different coloured belts the height of my focus. I could now clearly see their top buttons and even their epaulettes!

Then it was down the Tube and a noisy, clanking journey to what used to be our regular sleeping station. The old nightmares got to me when we

*Pentonville Prison – probably minus a few cons. (Islington Libraries)*

alighted at Caledonian Road. The platform was dim and almost deserted. The smells were still the same and I could still vividly visualise the rickety old double bunks and the hundreds of men, women and children sitting there with fear in their eyes as the sirens wailed and the dull thud as the bombs hit the ground. I wondered how many of them had survived the terrible pounding they had endured.

The once-familiar walk down Roman Way, past Pentonville Prison to my Nan's house in Offord Road, wasn't familiar to me any more. I didn't recognise anything except the prison walls on the right. My young eyes, now accustomed to clear, marvellous scenic views of the countryside and the beaches couldn't comprehend the scenes of utter devastation they witnessed. Whole streets had been razed to the ground, with just the odd wobbly wall or two standing upright – almost like mournful monuments to those poor innocent souls who had perished under the hail of German bombs. There was rubble everywhere; a strong acrid smell of burning

*Home again to a strange London. (Islington Libraries)*

wood permeated the air. Mum quickened her step and we all knew she was worrying about her parents. As we turned left into Offord Road, however, we saw that our Nan's side of the road was basically intact, yet the other side had been blasted to the ground. Living through the Blitz must have been the most terrible and frightening lottery to endure. If you were lucky, the next street copped the bombs and your neighbours were either killed, maimed or bombed out and you survived for another day. If you were one of the many unlucky ones, then mercifully you didn't know too much about it in the end. We cockneys have a wonderful saying that covers that scenario almost to perfection: 'If your card is marked . . .'. I believe it comes from racing slang.

Nan, Grandad and a couple of my aunts came out to greet us with lots of hugs and kisses. My Nan Rosie was a real character, a cockney through and through and tough as old boots. A big lady with a big face, she always wore a flowery apron and always kept her fags in the front pocket. She

*Left to right: Mum, Nan and Auntie Queenie. (Joan Westmore's collection)*

must have been a tough old bird, because many years later I discovered that every time she gave birth, one of her legs had to be broken; she bore eight children! My Mum, Rosie, was the eldest, but as I mentioned earlier, she was a 'lovechild'. The other three girls were Rene, Queenie and Edie. The four boys were Alfie, who was killed in the Desert War; Billy, who died soon after the war from cancer, then Harry and Lenny. My old Grandad Bill was also a right character. He was the exact opposite to my Nan, small and wiry, with piercing blue eyes and a bit of grey curly hair on the sides of his head, augmented by an imposing, grey walrus moustache. He also had a gammy leg – I think it was a legacy from the First World War. But, like most other cockneys, he never moaned and just got on with it. He'd worked all his life as a porter down at the old Covent Garden market, as did his sons after the war. And when he became too old and frail for humping all those boxes of fruit and veg around, they found him a job as a part-time cart-minder right opposite the old Floral Hall in Bow Street, now part of the newly refurbished Royal Opera House. Later on, I clearly remember jumping on one of the old trams at the Angel and popping down the Garden to see my uncles and my old Grandad. As

*Uncle Harry (centre) was a Desert Rat in Egypt. (Joan Westmore's collection)*

*Grandad's last journey. (Joan Westmore's collection)*

usual, I was on the cadge for a couple of apples or oranges, or anything that was going for that matter! But I did enjoy talking to my Grandad and stroking the old horses in his care. He was such a gentleman, he never raised his voice in anger. I think he earned his wages with tips from the buyers and cart-owners. In all honesty, it was one of the many made-up jobs by the closed-shop union to help out the old boys. The market unions and the porters always looked after their own in those days.

I was getting plenty of hugs and kisses from my aunts, especially from my favourite, Auntie Queenie. Her full 'title' was actually Queenie-Minny-Liza-Ellen. I suppose in today's parlance she would be called a bit of an old slapper, or even a good-time girl. But I thought she was gorgeous with her dyed, permed, curly blond hair, the black mascara on her eyes, the white make-up and the vivid red slash of lipstick across her mouth. I recall once reading a very funny description of the late Dame Barbara Cartland's make-up by some feature writer. I think she said that her eyes resembled 'two large blackbirds nesting on the white cliffs of Dover'. That was my Auntie Queenie down to a tee. She reeked of cheap perfume and whenever she went out, she always, but always had the dead foxfur around her neck with the beady little glass eyes staring at you!

''Ave a look at the bleedin' size of him, Mum,' said my Auntie Queenie to our Nan, while cuddling me into her ample bosom. 'I reckon our Alfie will be taking me down the Offord Arms very soon for a large port and lemon.' This brought roars of laughter from my Nan and Grandad and aunts before my Auntie Edie, who lived upstairs in Nan's house and had a stutter, said: 'L-l-leave 'im alone, Queenie, you're m-m-making 'im bl-bl-bleedin' blush.'

It seemed like forever that we lived with our Nan and Grandad before the house we were promised was ready. But it was great fun because they certainly knew how to have a good time. All us kids used to stand outside the local pubs most of the evening, while our relatives were boozing away inside. Every so often, one of them would appear with some lemonade or a bag of crisps to keep us happy until chucking-out time. When the grown-ups came out of the pub, you always knew when it was party time and time for a knees-up, because the men would all come out loaded up with crates of beer. They were joined together – almost like a daisy chain and spread across the road – all laughing and joking and puffing away on their fags. I distinctly recall it was a dozen bottled half pints in the big wooden crates and four big quart bottles in the little square crates. And, if you were ever invited to help carry the crates, that meant you were close to becoming a man and nearing the 'inner circle'!

Then it was back to our Nan's and someone used to start playing the old piano. Funny that, they didn't have two halfpennies to rub together, but they still had an old Joanna. Somebody else would get out the silly hats from some hidden place and start singing and playing party games. The hats were something else: sombreros, fezzes from Egypt and Australian bush hats, probably brought home by the returning soldiers. The silly games were taken really seriously, the ladies on one team and the men on the other. Two big beer mugs were placed at the end of the room and the contestants had to place a large coin in their buttocks. The object of the game was to hop the length of the room, then drop the coin into the beer mug. If you dropped it, you had to start again before the next player could begin. Obviously with everyone a bit sloshed the game went on and on until the contestants collapsed with laughter and exhaustion! One of the next-door neighbours had a regular party game that he always performed at every knees-up and it would bring the house down. Believe me, all he did was to tie a piece of string around the carcass of a chicken, or some other dead beast, and pull it around the parlour, scolding it and talking to it like a dog. So, if ever I heard the shout of 'Charlie, innit abaht time that bleedin' old dog of yours had its evening walkabaht?' I would scarper

*Devastation just around the corner from us. (Islington Libraries)*

*Kings Cross took a battering. (Islington Libraries)*

upstairs and lie on the bed with the pillow over my ears to shut out the sound. It was quite funny the first time around, but once you'd seen it and heard it half a dozen times, it wasn't funny anymore. It was only much later that I found out that Charlie had lost his wife and kids in an air raid and playing silly-buggers helped to keep him sane. I was told when the war was nearly over that poor old Charlie had finally joined his loved ones when he copped it with the very last doodlebug to fall on London. Somehow I don't think dear old Charlie would have minded in the least.

Although the war was still going on and every now and again we would hear a distant explosion as Hitler's new terror weapon, the V2 rocket, came down upon some poor souls, us kids still roamed the streets in the daylight hours. A nice little earner for me and my mates was to cadge

*The Archway after the Blitz. (Islington Libraries)*

*Clearing up the Archway. (Islington Libraries)*

a bucket and shovel off my Nan and collect the horse droppings in the surrounding roads. The streets around Offord Road weren't short of horse droppings, because it was a well-used route from the Kings Cross goods depot through to the City. Then we'd flog the manure to one of the big posh houses with a garden and there were plenty of them. Our 'manor', Islington, was a strange sort of area during the war. Most of it was made up of poor, working-class families and many of the big, posh houses had seen better days. But it was obvious that between the wars it had been an affluent place to live. Sir Basil Spence, the famous architect of the new Coventry Cathedral, was probably the first to make Islington trendy during the 1950s when he settled in Canonbury Square. Tony Blair and his family arrived in the same square much later. A few years after the war

*Destruction in Islington caused by V1s and V2s. (Islington Libraries)*

*Finsbury Park was hit hard. (Islington Libraries)*

*Another Islington pub bites the dust. (Islington Libraries)*

ended, the house prices in the area shot through the roof, especially when the professional people realised the potential of its close proximity to the City. The large house where my mate and his family lived in Belitha Villas was offered to his dad after the war for about two grand. But ordinary working people couldn't get mortgages on their meagre wages in those days and he had to turn down the offer. Some time later, living as sitting tenants, they were offered a brand new rented flat if they would move out. Their old house was then converted into four flats and each flat fetched more than £100,000 on the spiralling property market. Even our old dilapidated house where we moved to in Twyford Street became worth a lot of money, considerably more than the £400 my old Dad could have picked it up for after the war. But £400 then was the equivalent of around £40,000 today. A lot of people were making an awful lot of dough by refurbishing and flogging old properties.

But messing about on the roads with a bucket and shovel was a dangerous game, even in those times with very few cars about. One day I was knocked over by a car, just around the corner from my Nan's house. The driver was a really nice guy and drove me home because he was genuinely concerned. But he was bang out of luck because my old Dad opened the door and when he heard the story from the driver, you could see the sight of pound notes in his eyes. 'Well, guv,' said my Dad, 'I'll need to take your details and get my boy checked out right away down the doctor's.' The driver, a real toff, was shifting around in an uncomfortable way from one leg to the other. Who knows, maybe he had been visiting a lady friend on the quiet or something, but he was certainly nervous and jumpy. 'My dear chap,' he muttered, reaching into his inside pocket and pulling out a big, fat wallet. He opened it up to reveal a large wad of white fivers. 'Maybe we can settle this without involving the police. After all, it was only a minor incident.' 'I don't know about that, guv,' said my Dad. 'Wot if my boy's got brain damage?' The toff let out a big sigh and a look of annoyance came into his eyes as he said testily, 'I would think it highly unlikely your son was suffering brain damage, seeing as how my car only hit his leg.' But my old Dad was adamant, he was a cunning old dog and he knew that if the toff was offering dough he had something to hide, and Dad wasn't going to be bought off with a couple of fivers. 'Just give me your details guv and I'll pretend I didn't see you trying to bribe me,' he said. The toff knew he had met his match against an old, streetwise geezer on the make. He gave my Dad his business card and walked off in a huff. So I was dragged down the local doctor's the next day and told what to say. 'I keep getting these blinding headaches with terrible pains in the neck ever since my terrible accident and I can't sleep at night!'

Some weeks later my Dad told me I had to see a specialist down Harley Street and if I told a convincing tale about my 'blinding headaches' and the 'terrible pains in the neck', we would cop a nice few quid from the insurance company. So I rehearsed and rehearsed my story over and over again. Just a few days before seeing the top man at Harley Street, I 'bunked' into the pictures with some of my mates. They were showing some corny horror film about a monster with a great big head, great big hands and great big feet. I remember the scientist in the film saying very dramatically that the monster was suffering from 'acromegaly'. The dictionary describes this as 'a chronic disease characterised by enlargement of the bones of the head, hands and feet. This is caused by excessive secretion of growth hormones by the pituitary glands'. Funny what the mind stores up, isn't it? I've remembered that word for over sixty years and it still fascinates me!

So a few days later, off I goes with my Dad to the man at Harley Street. As I was ushered into a room I noticed two old blokes in white coats looking at me. One of them said to the other in a thin, reedy, posh voice. 'Not acromegaly, but slightly acromelagic, don't you think Mr Brown?' 'Mmm,' mused the other old bloke staring closely at me as if I was some sort of specimen. 'You could be right, Mr Smith.'

I can still recall the look of total disbelief on their faces to this very day when I snapped back at them. 'For your information, matey, I was born with a big bonce, and it ain't got nuffing to do with acromegaly or my accident.' The two of them were utterly speechless. How could this scruffy, backstreet urchin on an obvious insurance fiddle, possibly know about such a rare disease? These two consultants were completely bewildered and it was a joy for me to see them floundering. Suffice to say, they didn't believe one little bit of my cock and bull story about blinding headaches and severe neck pains, so my old Dad never got a penny. He should have cut his losses and taken the money he was offered in the first place. It doesn't pay to be too greedy! As the old saying goes: 'Little fish are sweet!'

Finally, and after what seemed an eternity, it was time for us to move on. I thought I heard our Mum telling Nan that we were moving to no. 2 Hyphen Street, but when I told this to Auntie Queenie, she fell about laughing. ''Ere,' she said to Auntie Edie, 'where d'ya think little silda-paper finks he's moving to?' She called me that because I couldn't pronounce 'silver paper' when I was a nipper. 'Go on, Alfie,' she said, 'tell your Auntie Edie where you're a moving to.' 'We're gonna live at no. 2 Hyphen Street,' I said, not knowing why she was laughing. 'N-n-no, Alfie,' said my auntie with the stutter. She started to stutter even more as the tears of laughter ran down her face. 'You're m-m-moving t-t-to T-t-twyford Street and its n-n-number b-b-bleedin' s-s-seven.'

The two of them fell about in fits of laughter, with tears streaming down their faces. I didn't think it was that funny, but they seemed to think so! As for me, I continued to tell all and sundry that I lived at no. 2 Hyphen Street. Who knows, if I had put that address down on my call-up papers when they arrived on my doorstep some seven years later, maybe I wouldn't have had to endure two years of National Service in the RAF. But that's another story for another book and you can read about it in *Bad Lads*!

Auntie Edie with the stutter lived on the top floor of my Nan's house in Offord Road with her husband Bert and their rather plump son, Michael. They were certainly a mismatch as a couple. Auntie Edie was tall and skinny, with funny glasses and Uncle Bert was quite the opposite. He was a dapper dresser and could almost be described as raffish. He had light ginger hair, plastered flat on his rather prominent head with Brylcreem. He sported a neat ginger moustache and had freckles on his fattish face. And he invariably wore nice suits with red braces that led down to a large beer belly. I liked Uncle Bert and I think he liked me, because he knew I was a ducker and diver, just like him. I recall once I admired one of his suits and he said, puffing away on his big cigar, with a twinkle in his eyes: 'First impressions go a long way in this world son and people like to see a nice whistle being worn by someone they're doing business with. So always remember boy,' he went on expansively, 'when you grow up you gotta hit them with that first impression.'

As I mentioned before, all my other uncles, and my Grandad before them, worked down Covent Garden as market porters. But not Uncle Bert, he was a costermonger through and through. I looked up that word recently and discovered it originated centuries ago and came from the word 'costard' meaning a large ribbed apple. The word 'monger' comes from the Old English word 'mangere', meaning a merchant. Thus the word costermonger is a compound word meaning a street merchant who sells apples! London's Pearly Kings and Queens originated in about 1886 and they all came from London's vast number of costermongers.

Back to my Uncle Bert, the costermonger. He had a fruit and veg stall down by the Arsenal ground in Holloway Road, right on the corner of Palmer Place, next to the Arsenal Café. One Friday, he said to me right out of the blue while I was playing in the garden: 'D'ya wanna help me out on the stall tomorrow, Alfie?'

This was music to my ears. I was bored, always getting into trouble and driving my Mum mad. Maybe my Mum had chatted him up to ask me, I wonder? 'Not 'arf, Uncle Bert,' I shouted out happily. 'Alright then, Alfie,' Uncle Bert said. 'I'll give you a shout early tomorrow morning – and I mean early!'

So bright and early the next morning, I set of with Uncle Bert to pick up all his gear. We walked up Offord Road, turned left into Westbourne Road and right into Mackenzie Road then left into Lough Road, next to the railway lines. I distinctly remember that opposite his lock-up there was a black wooden tower, almost like some sort of grain silo. Written on the black tower in huge white swirly writing were the words, 'Turner Byrne and John Innes, Grain Merchants and Cattle Feed'. Why I should remember that after more than sixty years, God only knows. Uncle Bert opened some iron gates with a big bunch of keys, walked into the yard and there was the head of a horse poking out of the stable door. I was so thrilled! I didn't even know Uncle Bert had a horse. 'This is Daisy,' said Uncle Bert, rubbing the horse's nose gently. 'And this is Alfie,' he went on, pulling me over so I could rub her nose. 'Just keep talking to her, Alfie, and keep stroking and patting her so she gets used to you,' said Uncle Bert. 'I'll get her out and we'll hitch her up to the cart, then we'll put her nosebag on so she can have some grub.'

Uncle Bert led out this beautiful brown horse with the white flash on her nose, hitched her up to the cart and gave her the nosebag. I was delegated to load on all the boxes of fruit and veg from the shed. It was hard work, but I was loving it all in the knowledge that I'd be riding on the cart soon. Uncle Bert took off her nosebag, clambered up on the cart, grabbed the reins and shouted out to me: 'Come on Alfie, up you get a bit lively.' What a great adventure! I climbed up on the cart and Uncle Bert made a sort of clicking noise with his mouth. He tapped Daisy lightly on the back and she walked out of the yard. 'Just hold the reins lightly, Alfie, and I'll lock up,' said Uncle Bert jumping down. I just sat there holding the reins, thrilled to bits.

What a great way to spend a Saturday. Out came Uncle Bert, jumped up on the cart, made that funny clicking noise again and off we went heading for Holloway Road. This was really living! We did a left turn into Mackenzie Road, crossed over Liverpool Road into Palmer Place, passing the huge emergency water tank, now the site of a church, and stopped on the right by the corner of Holloway Road. 'You lead her around the corner on the bridle, Alfie, and I'll start setting up the stall,' said Uncle Bert. So, I jumped gingerly off the cart, grabbed hold of Daisy's bridle, stroked her nose and tried to make that clicking noise like Uncle Bert. Bless her, she let me lead her round the corner by the stall – as good as gold! So, I stroked her again, called her a good girl and put her nosebag back on.

Now the real hard graft began. Uncle Bert put on his garish flat cap, which was almost the colour of his hair and moustache – a sort of gingery tweed. Then, on went his big apron with the zips across the front to hold the notes. And on some upturned boxes by the front of the stall, he put out the cash till. Well it wasn't any sort of till that the kids of today would recognise – or even many adults. It was just a lovely shiny block of wood and on the top, someone had carved out three circular holes that were about four inches deep. The biggest hole was about six inches across and the other two were about half that diameter. The holes themselves were curved and all smooth and shiny. 'Right Alfie,' said Uncle Bert pointing to the till, 'always remember to put the shrapnel in the big hole, all the tosheroons and the two-bobs in one of the other holes.' 'Okay Uncle Bert,' I replied knowingly. Then I had a thought. 'So where do I put the tanners or the joeys? 'Don't act dopey Alfie,' said Uncle Bert, with a look of disdain on his face. 'Think abaht it son, if you've got the bleedin' two bobs and tosheroons in one hole and the shrapnel in the other, you've only got one bleedin' hole left for the tanners and the joeys ain't ya?' 'Yeah, sorry Uncle Bert,' I replied with a hang-dog expression on my face. 'I just didn't want to mess it up early on and get a rollicking.' Uncle Bert looked up and smiled across at me with a twinkle in his bright blue eyes as he heaved up a sack of potatoes. So, I knew everything was alright and I was forgiven for being a dummy!

Working on a fruit and veg stall was totally alien to me, as I had yet to learn all the slang names for the produce. Uncle Bert would suddenly shout across to me: 'Alfie, we're running low on "new pots".' Then he'd shout out loudly for another tray of 'toms' or 'mush' or half a dozen punnets of 'straws' – they were the little boxes of strawberries. But what fascinated me the most was to stand behind him when he was adding up someone's bill – it was almost like a foreign language. 'Now, let's have a tot-up darling,' he used to say to some old biddy. 'The pots are a joey, the greens are a deuce, and the old apple and pears come to a tanner. So, the old Jack and Jill with all your other bits and pieces, comes to a kybosh.'

My Uncle Bert's expertise at slang expressions and rhyming slang never failed to amaze me. I used to earwig him talking to his fellow stall-holders. 'Naw, the gear's getting a bit pricey now down the Garden,' he would say, puffing away on his cigar. 'I paid a pony for my gear this week, yet last week it was only a score. My Jack and Jill came to a bottle this month and that was a score more than it stood me last month I went there.' 'The trouble is, Bert,' said one of the other costers, 'the punters round this manor ain't got the readies to pull up for any extras, 'cos most of 'em are on the Rock and Roll. So you can't up the ante, otherwise you'll get lumbered with all the gear'. 'Naw, you're right Harry,' said Uncle Bert. 'But you've only got to go up West and the punters down there ain't short of a few bob; I reckon we're working the wrong pitch.' They all nodded sagely in agreement and carried on puffing away on their fags and drinking their Rosie Lees. Later in the morning, Uncle Bert looked at his watch and shouted out at me. 'Strewth, Alfie, look at the bleedin' time, take a dinar out of the till and tell Carlos in the café we want two cheese rolls and two large Rosies. He knows who you are 'cos I told him about you earlier.' 'Okay Uncle Bert,' I said, taking the shilling out of one of the holes. 'I won't be a tick.'

I walked into the Arsenal Café and saw this foreign-looking bloke behind the counter pouring tea from a huge, stainless steel pot that looked almost as big as his little head. 'Two teas and two cheese rolls please, Mr Carlos,' I said politely. He looked up at me from beneath his big, bushy eyebrows and said in a voice that reminded me of the old gangster films. 'You got-ta be Bert's a-nephew Alfie, is that-a-so?' I nodded back and said: 'That's right Mr Carlos.' 'Hey Momma,' he shouted out. 'Come-a-see little Alfie, who-sa Bert's-a nephew.' The beaded curtain behind the counter was suddenly pushed open and out bustled a little, plump lady wearing a black frock with a white apron. 'He look-a-like a big strong boy, Pappa,' she said, flashing a big, toothy smile. 'You like-a helping your Uncle on his a-stall, Alfie?' 'Yes thank you, Mrs Carlos,' I replied. 'I really enjoy it.' She let out a loud giggle and both she and her husband looked up at the skies with their hands in the air and started saying something like 'Mamma Mia.' 'No, no Alfie,' she said, still laughing. 'That's-a Carlos Fellucci, she said pointing at her little husband, and I am-a Maria Fellucci from Italy.' I thanked them, still not knowing why they were laughing, picked up the teas and the cheese rolls and took them back to Uncle Bert.

But I was confused. 'Can I ask you a question, Uncle Bert?' He nodded, so I said, 'How come the Italians were on Jerry's side, yet Carlos and his missus are both Italians living over here?' He smiled, put down his cheese roll and his tea and, putting his thumbs into his bright red braces, said in an unusual, solemn voice. 'Let me explain son. Carlos and his family have lived over in London for donkey's years. He's probably more cockney than most of my punters and he's a long-time Arsenal supporter as well. Now we're all mates again.' He took another big puff on his cigar, stared me straight in the face and went on. 'Wot you 'ave to keep remembering when you grow up, is to make up your own mind about people and not listen to all that crap turned out by different governments who don't know what they are a-talkin' abaht. Take Adolf Hitler, as an example. If you woz to listen to 'im talking his crap, you wouldn't like anyone in the whole bleedin' world unless they were Jerries.' Yet another cloud of cigar smoke wafted over me, as he continued a costermonger's in-depth appraisal of world politics and the human race. 'Not all Italians are bad, the same as not all Jerries are bad,' he said. 'But there again, not all the English people are kosher. So you gotta learn to judge people yourself, Alfie.' He wasn't wrong, my Uncle Bert. As you make your way through life you learn to pick out some of the things that make sense. And, my Uncle Bert made good, down-to-earth common sense!

After a long, long day, Uncle Bert looked at his watch and said: 'Okay Alfie, it's time to shut up shop and get home and have some grub.'

*Alfie the teenager. (Joan Westmore's collection)*

So, once more I loaded the cart and Daisy took us back to Uncle Bert's lock-up. I can always remember her big, shiny back moving from side to side as she walked home. I helped to unharness her, put her in her stable and made sure she had plenty of food and clean straw. My reward for the day was a carrier bag of fruit and veg, known to all the market porters as a cochell, plus a half-crown coin for my day's labour! But again, the spending value of that half-crown in those far-off days was enormous. It would take me to the pictures – trouble was, me and my mates used to bunk in without paying anyway! But it certainly bought me plenty of sweets and chocolate on the Black Market because of rationing and lots of bags of chips!

My Saturday job lasted for quite a few weeks and I finally had the ultimate joy of driving the cart by myself. Uncle Bert turned round to me suddenly one day and said: 'Alfie, we're running low on pots and greens, 'ere's the keys and don't be too bloomin' long.' Sitting up on the high seat with the big brake pedal under my sole and talking to Daisy as we made our way back to the lock-up was my idea of heaven. I didn't want anything else. All the local kids were staring at me and I felt like a king for the day. I would have done this job for nothing – especially when some of the pretty local girls came a-running alongside the cart, all asking for a ride!

But sadly, it all ended soon after when we moved out of our Nan's house and settled down in Twyford Street and Uncle Bert's podgy son Michael took over from me. My apologies to Michael for calling him podgy if he happens to read this book. I've no doubt he is now a slim, handsome guy in his mid-sixties! Those were happy days on the stall and memories I will never forget.

Soon after that, my Uncle Bert and his family also moved out of our Nan's house to a different part of London and I've never seen my Uncle Bert, Auntie Edie, or their son Michael since that day! Lovely memories though, and I'll treasure them forever!

At the outbreak of the Second World War, Nicolette, my lovely wife for the past five decades, was living with her mother and baby sister in Holford Square, just off Kings Cross Road. It was just under a mile from where I was living. Her father was a regular in the army and one of the first to volunteer for the SAS when it was formed.

During the early days of the Blitz, all the families in the area regularly used the communal shelter in the square. She recalls after one really heavy air raid, returning to their house to find it almost completely destroyed. She remembers seeing the old-fashioned stained-glass window above the street door amazingly still intact, but without the street door which had been blown off. She remembers peering into the passageway and

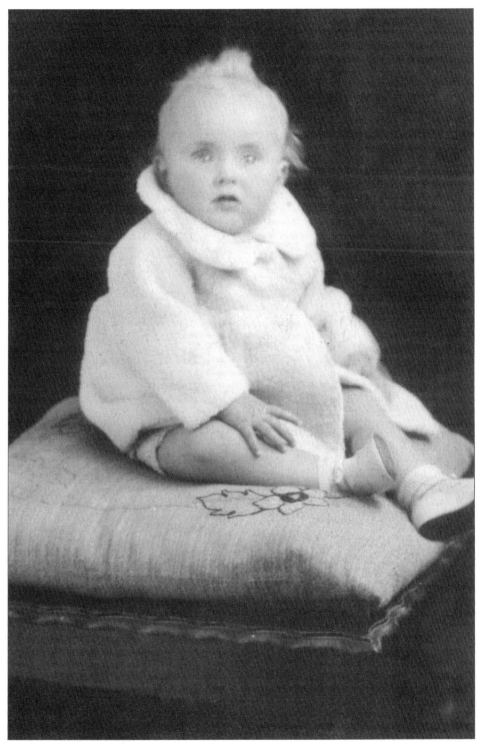

*My lovely wife Nicolette as a baby. (Author's collection)*

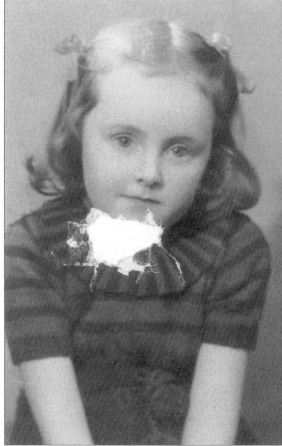

*Nicolette and her younger sister Rosalie. (Author's collection)*

*Nicolette as a youngster. The hole in the photograph was caused by shrapnel when bombs destroyed the house. (Author's collection)*

wondering why it was almost full to the ceiling with rubble. Her Mum had lost absolutely everything. The furniture was gone, so had all the kids' clothes. All of her Mum's precious bits and pieces of jewellery – even the linen and the kitchenware were destroyed. Worst of all, they had nowhere to live. They were bombed-out as the saying went in those days. But her little old Mum was feisty and resourceful. No way would Jerry beat her. So she attempted to salvage anything she could. Incidentally, the photo depicting Nicolette was actually on the mantelpiece when the bomb exploded and the hole was caused by a piece of shrapnel!

They loaded up an old pram to overflowing and trudged off through the rubble-strewn streets, all the way to one of her Mum's sister's place on the Crown Estate just off Albany Street, near Regent's Park. Again, while staying there, they took to using the communal shelter in the courtyard every night. Luckily for them, the only night they didn't visit the shelter it received a direct hit from a German bomb and many of their neighbours

*These lorries were not going anywhere! (Islington Libraries)*

*Nicolette and Rosalie again. (Author's collection)*

were killed. Like many other families, her Mum thought it would be safer to make the nightly trip to Euston Square Tube station. It was a bit of a drag, but well worth it. After many months of sharing an overcrowded flat with her aunt, they were finally given their own place on the Crown Estate.

While I was away, moving around the Cornish towns and villages, Nicolette and her family endured the worst of the Blitz. Her Mum tried desperately hard to keep the family together, but it was becoming increasingly difficult and dangerous. Nicolette's Mum was a dressmaker by trade and was forced to go to work in the rag trade centred around Great Portland Street, simply to feed and clothe her kids. By this stage of the war, Hitler was playing his last terror card against innocent and

*Not even churches were safe from the V weapons. (Islington Libraries)*

*More casualties and destruction in Islington. (Islington Libraries)*

helpless civilians. He launched thousands of rockets – firstly the V1s, then the V2s. 'V' was for vengeance, as the Nazis christened them, but they were nicknamed 'Doodlebugs' by the chirpy cockneys.

The V1 was in effect a flying bomb with a guidance system and a ton of high explosives packed into the front and propelled by a rocket. Some 7,000 of these flying bombs were aimed at London during the summer of 1944, with about 6,000 civilians being killed and many thousands injured. But the V1 had an Achilles heel. It could only fly in a straight line and even though it could reach speeds of 300mph, the British ack-ack batteries were shooting many of them down. The RAF, with their new Meteor jet fighters, could easily match their speed and destroy them. The young RAF pilots actually perfected a scheme where they would come alongside the V1 and give it a nudge on the wing. This had the effect of sending the V1 off course and hopefully making it crash into the deserted countryside.

The Nazis eventually produced a genuine rocket as a missile, the 'Vengeance Two' or the V2. The V2 had no military objective, it was set to come down anywhere in the London area. It flew at over 200mph and could reach its target in just four minutes. In November 1944, one of these V2s landed in the heart of New Cross, resulting in the loss of 160 innocent civilians. Eventually, after the successful invasion of Europe, the V2 sites were overrun and London and other British cities were finally safe. With the benefit of hindsight, it was just in time, because the Nazis were in the final stages of producing the world's first intercontinental ballistic missile, the A10. This had a range of 3,000 miles and could well have decimated all the American cities on the Eastern Seaboard or any other chosen targets of the Nazis. That would surely have necessitated negotiation.

Nicolette recalls how she and all the other London kids would be outside in the streets, happily playing on a fine summer's day and suddenly look up to the sky when they heard a deep, threatening roar. Then someone would spot the black shape of the V1 moving speedily through the cloudless sky, with the bright red flames belching out from behind. She remembers being almost mesmerised watching the rocket moving through the clear, blue sky and listening to that roar, a bit like a powerful racing car with a loud exhaust, she says. Then suddenly, a deadly silence ensued as the engine cut out, followed seconds later by an almighty explosion that shook the ground and rattled all the windows for miles around. Somewhere in the London area, dozens of innocent men, women and children had been killed or maimed by that terrible blast. The V1s and V2s really were terror weapons against the civilian population of our cities, simply because they weren't programmed for any specific or strategic target. They were just set to explode at random anywhere over the target city. I still remember how angry I felt after the war, when the Americans and the Russians were competing with each other to get the services of the best of the German rocket scientists to come and assist them with their space programmes. It still rankles me that these German scientists were fêted and treated like national heroes following the conquest of space. The Americans and Russians have short memories, mind you, they never had to endure these rockets crashing down on their own cities. To my simple mind, these scientists were responsible for the deaths of many thousands of innocent civilians in the terrible Blitz on the United Kingdom. Their inane excuse carries no more weight with me than the facile excuses offered by the major Nazi war criminals at the Nuremberg Trials that they were 'only carrying out orders'. How can perfectly normal human beings obey orders to liquidate six million Jews by gassing them?

Once the Doodlebugs started raining down on London, Nicolette's Mum decided it was too risky for her kids – especially because of their close proximity to the prime German targets of Euston, Kings Cross, St Pancras and Paddington stations. So, it became a regular weekend treat for them to get on a train and be taken for a ride into the country. Little did they realise that these weekend trips had a more serious purpose. Nicolette recalls her Mum checking addresses and knocking on doors in many little villages with lots of different ladies speaking to her Mum and shaking their heads. On some occasions, she remembers the ladies would point to her little sister Rose and say in a funny country accent. 'Oy'll take the little 'un, but oye can't take the two of 'em.' So her Mum would shake her head sadly and say with a big sigh: 'No, I'm sorry my girls are staying together – you either take them both or not at all.' Eventually, the girls were evacuated together to Rodmarton, a sleepy little village in Gloucestershire, for eighteen months.

Nicolette recalls that they were quite happy days living with a 'big fat, jolly lady' whose husband was in the RAF. She could never understand why, when he was home on leave, he would keep lying on top of the fat lady, still wearing his uniform, while the fat lady giggled heartily! It's an old country custom and very popular so I am told by 'Luscious' Liz, the receptionist at the History Press! I believe it's called Gloucestershire body wrestling! The hygiene in the house must have left a lot to be desired and within a short space of time, the two little girls were admitted to hospital covered from head to toe with scabby sores. They were diagnosed with impetigo. When their Mum arrived and saw the sorry state of her girls, she whisked them back to London and that truly ended their short and unhygienic evacuation.

Luckily for me, Nicolette survived the war and grew up to be a beautiful and lovely girl. We met at a Christmas dance at the old Hornsey Town Hall and danced to the crooning of my old mate Terry Parsons: it was love at first sight. Terry was on the buses at the Archway depot and he always sang in the local pubs like the Boston Arms in Junction Road and the Favourite in Hornsey Road. So one night, all of us chaps were at the Hornsey Town Hall, boozing away on our pints of brown and mild. Then the band-leader – I think his name was Fred Davies – got on the mike. His singer hadn't turned up and he wanted to know if anyone in the audience could knock out a decent song. So with plenty of pushing and shoving, we got Terry up on the stage. The rest is just like a fairy story. Terry had a great voice and was an overnight success. The famous band-leader Joe Loss signed him up and took him to a recording studio to make a demo tape. Luckily for Terry, one of the people involved in the recording was the very popular pianist, Winifred Atwell. She wasn't keen on his name and didn't think the tape would sell – even though she loved his voice. So they conjured up a stage name. The story goes that the sound man was called Matthew, so Terry became Matt and Winifred Atwell's old dad was called Monro. So Terry Parsons became Matt Monro and the rest is history. He went on to become one of the most popular British ballad singers of all time. I went past Terry once in my taxi as he was unloading his big flash American car outside Terminal One at Heathrow and shouted out, 'You alright Tel boy? Long time no see!' He looked up, smiled at me in a very special way and replied: 'Cor blimey, what a blast from the past, I ain't been called that name for years, Alf.' Tragically, Terry died far too young from a terrible disease he picked up on a tour of South Africa. Many people reckoned he was possibly Britain's greatest ever singer; even the late, great Frank Sinatra echoed those sentiments. Terry never thought he got the full recognition he deserved from the British public, even with his many hit records.

I know that the Second World War is almost ancient history to many people. But ask any person in their sixties or seventies who lived through the terrible Blitz in London what he or she remembers and the years will melt away, unveiling a vivid picture of the utmost clarity. Firstly, the really scary sound of the wailing sirens and the mad panicky dash for cover in the air-raid shelters. And then, the steady drone of the aircraft engines as you all huddled together, followed by the dull thud of the distant stick of bombs hitting the ground, creeping ever nearer and the acrid smell of burning that seemed to constantly permeate your nostrils. Us kids thought the grown-ups were so brave, yet they must have been more terrified than us. They were adult enough to understand the dangers and they knew that if Hitler had invaded Britain, with our limited resources in the early days of the war, he may well have made true his boast of 'marching down Whitehall'. Yet they would stand up and sing all their silly little songs down the Tube and in all the pubs about Hitler being 'a twerp', with great gusto. Then it was a noisy rendition of 'Pack Up Your Troubles In Your Old Kitbag', followed by all the Vera Lynn favourites, over and over again. If you had lived through those terrible, terrible times, it would stay clear in your memory until your dying day. Even now, while I'm bashing away on my computer late into the night, desperate to rid my mind of the demons from sixty years ago, the tears are streaming uncontrollably down my cheeks. It was all so horrific and the people of London were so terribly brave. I'm so proud to count myself as one of them. Please God, let the rest of the world wake up and react quickly whenever another ruthless dictator attempts to subjugate a whole race of people. Hindsight shows us that the Second World War could well have been avoided before Hitler got too strong and powerful. The policy of appeasement is fraught with dangers, as Prime Minister Neville Chamberlain and his cabinet discovered to their cost. Waving a piece of paper signed by Hitler doesn't mean a thing if it comes from a deceitful, lying person. The dictator needs a short, sharp lesson early on in the game to convince him that he can never win! That's why Winston Churchill – even with a dodgy track record – proved so popular with the British public and our allies. He could read Hitler like a book, in fact he was often one step ahead of him.

# EIGHT

# VICTORY IN EUROPE

It's hard to believe in this modern age of vehicle technology that my old Dad actually borrowed a coal cart to move all our stuff from our Nan's place in Offord Road down to Twyford Street! We turned into our new street, with the old-fashioned, red-brick building that was the Caledonian Road Public Baths and Wash Houses dominating the corner. Sadly, it is now replaced by an ugly modern effort. How many thousands of times had I whacked a football against that old red-brick wall? How many times, with the aid of a grappling hook and some rope, had our gang climbed the steep sheer sides to watch the boxing without buying a ticket? I thought the old Victorian terraced houses looked quite homely and comforting, but just as soon as you opened our front door, it was obvious that they were literally falling to bits. The hallway or passage of no. 7 had a gaping hole just inside the door and all the time we lived there, it was never repaired! To the right of the passage was the front room or parlour. This had a wonky sliding door that connected to what is now called the 'master bedroom'. At the end of the dark passage was the kitchen with a scullery and a door that led to an outside lavatory and a small, postage-stamp garden. Up the first flight of stairs was another small bedroom that I would share. But the whole place was dark, dank and dingy with no hot water and, would you believe, gas lighting! But, beggars can't be choosers and it was better than nothing.

Upstairs lived the old lady who my Mum had befriended and who owned the property. The old lady really scared the life out of us kids. She always wore the same, rather grubby Victorian-looking frock with a high collar and little lace-up boots. She never went out without wearing a hat but even her hats were weird, funny little numbers that seemed to perch unsteadily on her matted grey hair. What made us kids laugh was the huge, silver hatpin that held it in place. It looked for all the world that the hatpin had pierced one side of her head and come out the other side! When she suddenly died, my old Dad swore blind she had kept all her money sewn in that frock and that the undertakers had nicked it! That was after he had illegally searched her flat of course! The missing money was his constant topic of conversation for many years after, but sadly he was just a dreamer and spent most of his life talking about when 'his ship came home' and when 'he won the pools'!

By this time in 1945, I had been enrolled in Treaty Street School and was busy studying for the eleven-plus exam. Along with all the other working-class families in North London, we couldn't get any coal to keep us warm through the bitter winter of 1947 and we were absolutely freezing in the old damp houses. Even attempting to bribe the local coal merchant didn't do any good – there just wasn't any coal available for households. So one freezing cold day my Mum got out her old pram and told me to follow her down to the coal base. This was in Camley Street, just off Goodsway behind Kings Cross station where the open-sided coal trucks were shunted into sidings. So, off we went in the freezing cold. Up Twyford Street, left into Bemerton Street and right into Copenhagen Street, with my school towering above the totally devastated local streets – razed to the ground by a massive mine on a parachute. Even this terrible explosion and loss of life had a sad twist. Many of the young soldiers who were 'on the run' used to frequent the local pub on this site – I think it was called the Red Lion. They had deserted from the army – only to be killed while having a pint with their mates! Then we went left into York Way, over the canal bridge and right into Goodsway. This area became the favourite haunt of prostitutes in the 1950s and '60s.

The local coalies used to queue up alongside the trucks with their horses and carts, while railway staff loaded up the big, black smelly coal bags and weighed them before they were loaded onto the carts. Again, I was back to my favourite country pastime – another form of beachcombing. The cracks in the floors of the coal trucks enabled small pieces of precious coal to drop on the tracks and I would crawl underneath and attempt to fill my little sack before I was spotted. Mind you, I went to school with many of the coalies' kids – especially the Armsby Brothers – so they knew me quite well and often turned a blind eye to my capers. Then, we would load up the old pram with the spoils and trundle back home again and enjoy a few cosy nights around a red-hot fire. I happened to be in the the Goodsway area recently in my taxi and decided to go round to the old coal base in Camley Street and try to put some feeling into what I was attempting to write about. That turned out to be a total waste of time. The once-scruffy sidings had changed so dramatically, I honestly thought I was in the wrong place. The massive gasometers were still there, but the old railway lines had gone and it had now been converted into a pleasant, almost rural retreat, pleasantly landscaped with large trees growing where the sidings used to be. This overlooked a very picturesque stretch of the once foul and stinking canal.

*A teenage Alfie with sister Irene. (Author's collection)*

When our gang used to dive off the bridge in York Way on a fine summer's day, we encountered the bodies of dead dogs, cats and sometimes human remains! How we never caught some awful disease like typhoid I'll never know. How things change with the passing years! Even today, that area has again changed drastically with the massive, four-year redevelopment of St Pancras station for the arrival of the new Eurostar Service.

Being kids we made our own enjoyment and we had some good laughs – especially rummaging through the wreckage of shops. One such shop used to sell toys and I fondly recall digging up dozens of penny whistles. So, what on earth did I want with dozens of penny whistles you may be asking? I flogged them to other kids! Then, one day my old Mum told me that all the major film companies were starting a Saturday club for kids. This was an obvious attempt to get more bums on the seats. So off we all went down to the bus stop, clutching our sixpence entrance fee and jumping on a trolley-bus up Caledonian Road to the old Mayfair Cinema – now a block of luxury flats. Hundreds of wide-eyed, scruffy kids sat back in awe as the lights went out. Then it was sing-along time as the words came up on the screen and a bouncing ball literally bounced over every word.

*Centre stage in the Scouts gangshow. (Author's collection)*

We come along on Saturday mornings treating everybody with a smile
We come along on Saturday mornings knowing it's well worthwhile
As members of the GB Club we all intend to be
Good citizens when we grow up and champions of the free
We come along on Saturday mornings treating everybody with a smile,
    smile, smile, treating everybody with a smile

This hearty sing-along was followed by a Laurel and Hardy comedy, then a corny old Western, before the lights went on for the interval. We settled down expectantly for the second half of the programme and rocked in our seats at the antics of Abbott and Costello. Then came the big finish, the very first sci-fi movie to be made, our hero Flash Gordon. The producers always left poor old Flash Gordon in a truly desperate situation at the close of every episode – just to make sure you didn't miss the follow-up. I recall one time when Flash was locked in a room by the baddies and, at the turn of a switch, the room was getting smaller and smaller and crushing him. I remember I worried all the following week how he would escape! Finally, before the national anthem was played, another sing-song about road safety – again with the bouncing ball!

We must have safety on the King's highway, look right, look left, look
    right – and look left again
And off we go when the coast is clear, safely home to Mummy 'cos
    there's nothing to fear

Lovely old memories – and it beats watching the television all day!

Even I, as a ten-year old, realised that the war in Europe was quickly coming to an end. Grown-ups were constantly saying things like 'Jerry's on the run' and 'the Yanks are near Berlin'. And all the old biddies around our manor – well, they seemed old to me at the time – were forever going on that 'our boys will be coming home soon'. Then, soon afterwards, a strange thing happened. I heard all these sirens howling and hooters blowing and suddenly, all the street doors opened and people started running out into the road and hugging and kissing each other. They had obviously been listening to the wireless when they had announced that Germany had surrendered and the war in Europe was finally over. Not so the fanatical Japanese in the Pacific. It would take the total destruction of Hiroshima and Nagasaki by the dreaded A-bomb before they surrendered. But I was too young to comprehend what the grown-ups had had to suffer through the war years. The dread, coupled with the sadness of losing their husbands, wives, sons, daughters, brothers, sisters or loved ones in the terrible battles. The daily and nightly fear of the German bombs, landmines and Doodlebugs raining down on their houses, the constant knot in their stomachs that Hitler and his Nazi hordes could well have invaded Britain. All those years of anger, anguish and pent-up emotions were released by that mad rush out onto the streets and wildly dancing around kissing and cuddling anyone you saw. As for me, I thought they had all gone a bit potty!

Then it was time to help organise the VE Day street party. That was the joy of being part of a 'street family' in London after the war. For sure you didn't get on with all of your neighbours all of the time, but there was a feeling of warm security that permeated right through to every member, from the very young to the very old and infirm. And woe betide any outsider who had the audacity to take a liberty with any person in our street. Our top men would get it sorted a bit lively! This is how the retribution was handed out in the case of violence – or a liberty taken to one of our own. Find out the age of the perpetrator, whether he was a teenager, in his twenties, or even older. Then carefully select someone of the same age from our street who could handle himself in a punch-up and dispatch him to beat the shit out of the guy. A bit like the Mafia I suppose! Sadly, all these close-knit communities were completely decimated in the 1950s and '60s, long after I had moved away from the area to get married. Our local council decided to level the whole area to the ground and replace all the quaint, but solid, Victorian terraced houses with ugly flats and maisonettes that unfortunately have not stood the test of time. This massive building programme was particularly evident on 'our' side of Caledonian Road, starting from the canal bridge, right through to the dreaded Pentonville Prison, a distance of around half a mile. Strangely enough, the opposite side of the road, what we peasants termed as the posh side, was hardly touched. Those houses were somewhat larger, but many still needed to be replaced. In one fell swoop, whether by coincidence or deliberate design, the planners had completely decimated many close-knit communities that had lived together for decades. With their massive building project they had inadvertently created two completely diverse communities of the 'haves' and the 'have nots', with Caledonian Road separating them. Now, some sixty-odd years down the line the council side of the divide is looking decidedly scruffy and dilapidated, while the posh side is looking even posher after having been 'gentrified' by the mass arrival of professional people in the 1960s. Yet I find it a strange scenario whenever I take a fare in my cab to my old manor, albeit to the posh side of the divide. Even though these professional people have lived there, maybe for a generation or more, and lovingly cared for their houses, they can hardly be termed as part of the local community. I mean you'll never see them up Chapel Market buying their fruit and veg, or looking in some of the rather tatty shops up the Cally. But hey, I'm just telling my story, I'm not a social reformer!

But let's return to my helping to organise the VE Day street party. We Londoners are a strange lot – there's no doubt about it. The capital had been battered for five years by the heaviest bombing the world had ever witnessed, but never ever into submission. The whole of the population had existed on an almost starvation diet, with the growing kids never getting their proper vitamins from fruit and the like. But, give us the opportunity of a street party and the chance to cock a snook at 'Jerry', and the hidden goodies saved for a rainy day, suddenly appeared like magic. I remember our VE Day street party in Twyford Street as if it were only yesterday – probably because it nearly killed me – and I mean that literally. The tables and chairs were lined up half the length of the street and everybody wore home-made party hats and each household had to donate some sort of food. We had jellies and blancmanges and custard, loads of sandwiches and home-made cakes and fizzy drinks, while the grown-ups drank beer and cider.

'Jack the lad' on the left. (Author's collection)

The guys who worked down Covent Garden had come home with a nice cochell of fruit that I'd never seen before. As mentioned before, a 'cochell' was the slang term for the carrier bag full of fruit and veg that the market porters used to bring home at the end of the day. I think this practice went way back to the Victorian era. The guv'nors didn't scream about it, in case they got a major strike on their hands and the 'Beadles', the market security, turned a blind eye! Can you possibly imagine a kid of today not knowing how to eat a banana because he'd never seen one in his whole life? One of my mates was seen attempting to eat a banana – skin and all!

*Alf the teddy boy, front left. (Author's collection)*

The festivities went on to well after dark and the organisers turned on the old-fashioned spotlights. As usual, I was right up the front making a nuisance of myself, that's probably why one of the organisers said to me, 'Alfie, turn that spotlight round to face the tables, will ya?' So I went across and started pulling at this big old spot lamp and trying to heave it around. It probably wasn't even earthed properly and most likely had been set up by an amateur sparky. And that's all I can remember. There was just total blackness and I slipped into unconsciousness from a massive electric shock. More by luck than anything else, I eventually started to come round and I saw all these faces looking down at me. Someone was stroking my face with what I can distinctly remember was a cold, smelly flannel and I heard a man's voice say. 'Ain't nuffing wrong with 'im, he'll be alright.' And that was that. No doctor, no medic, no ambulance, no check-up at the local hospital, no nothing. I was quickly ushered back to the party and given an extra large lump of chocolate cake. That's obviously a very good cure for a massive electric shock! Medical researchers are now saying that an electric shock is good for the heart. Well, touch wood, up until now I am strong as an old ox! I recall that the next-door neighbour's pretty daughter Betty Tulip, was somewhat concerned about me. It appears that Mrs Tulip and my old Mum had agreed among themselves that me and Betty would make a nice couple in the future. But real life doesn't work out that way. I didn't fancy Betty and I don't think she fancied me! After I'd moved away from home I heard the tragic news that pretty Betty had died in a horrendous car accident. What a loss of a lovely young girl.

So, I had lived through some hair-raising experiences in the early days of the Blitz. I had survived some traumatic experiences as an evacuee. I had made it through the terrible rocket attacks and now I had survived a massive electric shock that could well have killed me. And with the same luck I could move on to manhood and a happy marriage with a lovely brood of kids and grandchildren. And that's just what happened! Yet even after all these years of being happily married, I still can't understand why a lovely convent-educated girl from a nice family should choose to spend her life with a rather pompous, loud-mouthed yob, dragged up in the post-war poverty of Caledonian Road. They say opposites attract and you just couldn't get more opposite than Nicolette and Alfie!

But my story simply cannot end there. For sure, I've brought it up to the present day, but it just can't end before returning to Newquay after over sixty years. I know the journey back in time will be painful and sometimes sad, and I know I'll be thinking: 'Is this the final time I'll see Newquay before I kick the bucket?' But hey, I'm always like that and my wife is fond of calling me an 'old drama queen!'

So we made the decision together, I needed to go back to Newquay, just for a couple of days, to check out all the changes. My dear wife Nicolette would come with me for moral support and together we would research the town and record everything for the final chapter! And that brings me neatly to the popular old American ballad from the war.

Gonna take a sentimental journey, gonna set my heart at ease.
Gonna take a sentimental journey to renew all memories.

## NINE

# NEWQUAY:
# SIXTY-ODD YEARS ON

I didn't really want to make the journey back after all those years. I was quite happy to bottle out and live with my boyhood memories – even though I had made them conveniently comfortable in my mind over the ensuing years. My dear wife, however, was adamant after I had changed my mind for the umpteenth time! 'We WILL go to Newquay together,' she snapped in a stern voice I hadn't heard since she scolded our youngsters many years ago, 'and the reason I will be accompanying you back to Newquay is because you have written a book that is incomplete and an incomplete book will not be acceptable to the publishers and will not be acceptable to the loyal readers of your first two books.' I just sat there, eyes agog and nodding, because when Nicolette goes off on one, you don't argue – in fact, you don't even dare to speak!

The journey back in time even started with a strange coincidence. In 1940 all of us kids piled into the lift at Caledonian Road station, totally unaware of the terrors facing us down on the platform. And now, all those years later, this septuagenarian and his lovely wife were doing exactly the same thing in the lift at the posh Hampstead station. I suppose if I had thought out the journey a bit better, I perhaps would have chosen a station on the Northern Line without a lift! It was a bad start for me. Suddenly my hands were getting a bit sweaty and my socks felt as though I was wading through our garden pond. The lift whirred to a halt and I shuffled out on to the platform feeling a bit queasy. After fifty years of being happily married, my wife can read me like a book and promptly handed me a tissue to dry my hands. 'This is as bad as flying for you luv, isn't it?' she said, trying to comfort me. I nodded nervously in reply. I hate flying – even though I was in the RAF. I hate lifts and I hate boats. In fact all I like is driving my own taxi!

I tried to bury my head in a newspaper and not look around. Even the pristine condition of the station wasn't enough to wipe the demons from my mind because the smells were the same as all those years ago. I just knew that if I looked up, I would see those old double-bunks again and the hordes of people milling around. Then I felt the rush of warm air and heard the loud rumble of the approaching train. I would have been quite happy to have gone back up in the lift and called the whole thing off – booked tickets or no booked tickets! I waited until the train screeched to a halt and the doors clattered open before I put my paper down – thinking that if I didn't look around it might help – and it did.

The journey to Paddington station wasn't too alarming for me. Mind you, I must confess to having a wobbler when we had to change at Kings Cross. This wobbler was threefold: firstly I was still worrying about the Blitz; secondly, thinking about the terrible loss of life in the ghastly Kings Cross fire; and, thirdly, recalling the vivid images of the dead and injured in the terrorist attack at the station on 7/7.

We walked briskly up the steps that took us to the middle of the station concourse at Paddington and the place was bedlam! One minute we were deep in the bowels of London with just the smell of the underground and the very next minute we had entered the hectic world of the morning commuters from all over south-west England! There were literally thousands of people around and apart from the lack of uniforms, it wasn't unlike 1940. But the station had changed radically over the years and like many other mainline stations, it still had the huge Victorian arches covered with glass. But the many thousands of panes of glass were now certainly much cleaner without the soot and steam from the old engines. In fact, there were no engine smells or smells of any kind! There were shops and cafés all over the concourse and big, shiny escalators to take you up to another level of even more shops and cafés. Being an old-fashioned bloke, probably living in the past, I had a bit of a shock when our bill for a sandwich and a couple of cups of coffee came to over a tenner! Another shock came when I went into the gents toilet. There was an iron turnstile and a sign saying: '20p access to the toilets and £3 for a shower.' I couldn't help but think: 20p for a pee, that's a bit strong isn't it? Then it was into the ticket office to see if OAPs got a discount.

Obviously, all the passengers looked different from all those years ago, hordes of tourists lugging huge cases – probably heading for the Heathrow Express. And isn't it easy to spot the mature American ladies? All rather on the large side with very prominent bottoms and all wearing their white trainers! There were lines of gents in smart suits striding past with a kind of glassy look in their eyes and lots of pretty young ladies. I paused to reflect for a moment before going nervously on to the platform. Hardly any of these passengers had even been born when me and thousands of other scared inner-city kids made our wartime journey down to Cornwall. The thought made me feel as though I was a stranger from another planet!

I chuckled to myself as I thought of Uncle Albert, the old sailor in the classic comedy, *Only Fools and Horses*. What if I was to grab hold of one of these glassy-eyed businessmen and simply say to him: 'During the war . . .', and then bore him to death with one of my stories?

Suddenly I was feeling a bit perkier and really looking forward to the long train journey back to my childhood. No sitting outside a stinking toilet this time around and the seats were booked. I had my notebook and my specs at the ready. We had pre-booked a charming little guest house – very close to Stanley Cottages and the harbour – our first home in Newquay, so everything was going swimmingly!

It was the morning rush-hour but luckily we were heading against it. But as we went on to the platform to board our train, one of the commuter trains pulled up on the other side and disgorged an amazing number of people. Suddenly we seemed to be facing a veritable army marching relentlessly towards us with the women seemingly holding their large handbags in an almost threatening manner! As for the pin-striped horde, they marched glassy-eyed – almost in formation. I had this vision of their umbrellas pointing forward like spears, holding their briefcases across their chests like shields! We moved nervously to the left well out of the way, otherwise we would have been squashed like ripe tomatoes!

Finally, we boarded our train pulled by a monstrous diesel locomotive. No posh names for these monsters anymore like 'The Brighton Belle' or 'The Flying Scotsman', just a workmanlike 'Stroud 700'. And thankfully no more old-fashioned corridors, so no having to sit on a battered suitcase outside a stinking loo! Comfortable, open-plan carriages and tables and cosy seats were the order of the day. But what a drastic change of scenery since arriving at Paddington all those years ago! As we pulled out of the station I saw that the massive bomb damage had now been replaced by a multitude of huge towerblocks that reared their ugly heads either side of the track for miles. But soon we were speeding through the lovely English countryside. No more loud clanking over badly fitted track joints, just a pleasant humming sound that numbed your senses in a relaxing way. Bacon buttie and coffees in the buffet bar was enough to break the monotony until we reached Brunel's coastal track at Dawlish. That was something special and not to be missed. The red sandstone cliffs, the Exe and Teign rivers and the wonderful views of all the many ships bobbing about on the water, was a sight that brought back many old memories. Then onto the spectacular Tamar Bridge that separates Devon from Cornwall. I have to confess that it didn't appear to be quite so high this time around. But hey, I was only about six the last time and everything seems extra big when you are so low to the ground! An added attraction since the 1970s was a two-tier road bridge running alongside.

We changed at Par for Newquay. But this time around no stentorian voice on a crackly old loudspeaker naming all the stations down the line in a strong Cornish accent. Just an announcement on the train intercom by one of the lady staff. We crossed the bridge for the Newquay train, just one small carriage with a handful of passengers and headed for our final destination. The deep cuttings and the sinister overhanging trees were as I remember them and the white 'mountains' still looked prominent – but strangely not quite as white. Mind you, having had sixty-odd years of vegetation growing on them, they wouldn't look as white, would they? Then the train slowed down as we crept across the wobbly old Trenance viaduct. As I looked down I could recognise the tennis courts, the lovely flowerbeds and the boating lake. I've since learned that this whole area used to be flooded by the River Gannel at high tide and was called the Old Moor. During the depression of the 1930s, local unemployed men were paid dole money, some tobacco and a pasty per day to dig out the boating lake. At the end of each week their wives were given a packet of tea, not a lot, but certainly better than starving!

We came to a halt and that meant I had finally returned to my boyhood after all those years. But I was rather confused. I had always pictured Newquay station in my mind as a buzzing hive of activity with hordes of people flocking around the four platforms and trains coming and going. Not any more. Most of the platforms had been concreted over leaving just the one. And as for the hordes of people, now it was just my wife and myself, plus a very old lady with a similarly ancient dog!

We came out of the station and I couldn't help but notice the Great Western Hotel almost opposite, one of the town's first major hotels. Back in the 1940s this grand hotel enjoyed almost total isolation and its creamy paintwork, elaborate classic design and wonderful sea views made it a must for the rich and wealthy. This is where the American officers stayed before D-Day and this is where I spent many a pleasant evening sneaking up and peering through the French windows at all the latest movies – not forgetting my gashed leg and being sewn up like a chicken by that American Angel. Now the view of the old hotel is almost obliterated by ugly buildings and, would you believe, a karaoke club! We turned left and headed for the town centre passing by my last home in Newquay, the Cliff Close Hotel, or rather where it used to be! Surprise, surprise, it had been demolished and in its place was a rather large pub and restaurant called Griffins. The other side of the old tramtrack where the American soldiers used to live, including my eldest sister's heartthrob the 'Mexican Bandit', was now a pile of rubble waiting to host yet another apartment block or

*Back at Newquay again – still with hair! (Author's collection)*

hotel. Straight down Cliff Road and we were in the centre of town. Lots of surfing shops, lots of bars and cafés and lots of amusement arcades. It could have been Brighton, or even Southend. No, definitely not Southend – they don't have breakers! The old Wesleyan chapel opposite Towan Beach, where I intermittently went to school, and where I got a whack around the ear from a teacher for cutting off all the tops of the lettuces with my hoe, is now, would you believe, a funeral parlour. The view across the Killacourt Green to the sea was still stunning, even though it had been intruded upon by an ugly block of flats that blocked the famous view of Jago's Island and its suspension bridge. Apparently, there has been a dwelling on this island from the turn of the twentieth century and its most famous resident was Alexander Lodge, the inventor of the Lodge sparking plug!

We walked past South Quay Hill by the harbour and I recognised the site of Stanley Cottages, our very first home in Newquay. Again this had been demolished and replaced by trendy arts and crafts shops. I was sad that it had gone, but thank goodness it hadn't been replaced by some ghastly amusement arcade! It was a brisk walk down Fore Street until we came to no. 92, Rockpool Cottage, our chosen home for the next few days. It's a funny old world isn't it? Out of all the many hundreds of hotels and bed and breakfasts in Newquay, we just happened to choose Rockpool Cottage on the internet. This place had a notorious reputation back in the 1960s and '70s when it was called the Yellow House. The Yellow House was the abode of hordes of young, beer-swilling, wacky baccy-smoking mad surfers of both sexes. In effect, it was probably one of the very first hippy communes totally devoted to the love of surfing. So when the present owner Craig Smithurst – himself a keen surfer – came down to Newquay from up north some thirty years ago, he never went back. He eventually purchased the house, which was in a terrible state. But by sheer hard work and a penchant for DIY, Craig has transformed the 'pits' into a 'palace'. Believe me, it's never a simple exercise when I travel – there's always a good story to be had! So we settled in after having a good meal and some drinks in the Red Lion pub and looked forward to our next day's exploration. I have to mention the superb view of the harbour from the lofty vantage point of the Red Lion, it really is like a picture postcard. I could pick out the steep wooded cliffs that we use to shin up for crab apples and, looking to the left by South Quay, was the bore hole through to Towan Beach. This is where our gang sat in nervous silence waiting for the tide to come rushing in. But after over sixty years of tides and rising sand, only the top 3 feet were now visible. But not much had changed about the harbour after all those years.

The next day dawned a bright and sunny October morning and, after a full English breakfast in our room, we were ready to go. We headed up Fore Street towards the five-star Atlantic Hotel on the headland. On the left of the hotel is the war memorial, commemorating all the Newquay men and women who died in both world wars. To the right and overlooking the harbour is the Huer's Hut. The huer was basically a lookout and as soon as he saw the distinctive ripple on the surface of the sea and the reddish purple hue just beneath the surface, denoting the approach of a shoal of pilchards, he would yell down a megaphone-like trumpet to the waiting fishermen. This cry of 'hubba, hubba' would spread throughout the locality, causing much excitement. Everyone would rush to the quay and to their boats, urged on all the while and guided by their huer. Each fish cellar had its own huer and competition was fierce.

Then we turned left and followed the clifftop path up to the impressive Headland Hotel. I can distinctively remember this hotel during the war. An imposing red-brick Victorian edifice that I always thought looked like a lunatic asylum! The building of this hotel was completed in 1900, even though there were riots from the locals. For generations, local fishermen had dried their nets and grazed their sheep on this headland and they felt very angry about many areas of Newquay being snapped up by property speculators. But since the coming of the railway, the landed gentry and well-to-do visitors demanded high-class hotels in which to stay. In 1911, Edward, the Prince of Wales, himself stayed there while convalescing from a bout of measles, thus attracting the wealthy from all over the country and ensuring that Newquay developed into a thriving holiday resort.

After reaching the end of the headland and taking in the Old Coastguard Station and the Old Lifeboat House, we turned left again towards the famous surfing Mecca of Fistral Beach and past the once-familiar golf

*A pensive Alf looking out over Fistral Beach. (Author's collection)*

*Alf, the casual observer, above Great Western Beach. (Author's collection)*

links of my boyhood. I have since discovered that the links are on the site of an old commercial lead mine. Finally, we reached Pentire Road close to the Pentire Hotel where I spent many happy months with my family and the buxom matron. What caught my eye were the dozens of notices all over the place saying 'No camping, no cooking and no sleeping overnight'. I can well imagine all the aggravation the local residents had in the past with the young surfers and beach-bums until the council sorted it out!

But by far the biggest surprise on my journey back in time was to see the massive amount of building all over Pentire Head. Okay, so I didn't expect to see the same desolate, scrubby headland with a few dilapidated cottages dotted about. But neither did I expect to see every inch of it completely covered with hotels, apartments and houses of all shapes and sizes. Even areas that I remember as green fields, with cows and sheep grazing in them, have now been turned into high-class housing developments and still the building goes on! Our old home, the Pentire Hotel, was no more and is now a posh, new apartment complex with a rather ridiculous Spanish-sounding name. The old-fashioned lamp post, where my American buddies placed their candy collection, had been replaced by one of those modern things with sodium lighting. As for the old view from my bedroom window down the once deserted U-shaped lane where my American friends arrived before D-Day. Sadly, like every other little country lane on Pentire, it has been turned into a residential street with houses, hotels and apartment blocks on either side. In retrospect, I suppose it was inevitable with the increasing popularity of Newquay over the many years since I left.

Finally, it was to my boyhood retreat, the River Gannel. It's still a wonderful sight to see from the steep and rocky footpath that leads down the side, although it appears that the developers are doing their utmost to obliterate the public right of way to this outstanding scenic

*Going to the Gannel.*
*(Author's collection)*

*Gazing out to the Gannel. (Author's collection)*

view. During the war – I'm sounding like Uncle Albert again, aren't I? – I often visited the two-masted schooner that was moored on the other bank, in between my spear fishing of course! The *Ada* was a museum of curios and American servicemen stationed further up the Gannel used to flock to the ship paying a shilling a time to see the exhibits. At the peak of its popularity, there were as many as 100 visitors a day. The old ship finally came to its end in 1951. She was sold for a paltry £40 and much of her pitched pine decks were removed, before she was set alight. Locals say the *Ada* burned for two whole weeks!

*The author at his Hampstead home – well the top flat, anyway! (Author's collection)*

And that was just about that. We took the same scenic walk back over the cliff path and a tasty dinner and drinks at the Red Lion. Then a good night's sleep, followed by another full English breakfast, and it was time to take the same walk back to the station. What struck me about Newquay was the preponderance of sparrows – they are all over the place. The dear old cockney sparrow may have left its home in London, but they are alive and kicking in Newquay!

So, was my journey back to my boyhood after all that time away worth the effort? The answer is most definitely yes, because it has enabled me to finally exorcise the perennial demons in my head that have haunted me since childhood. I can now comfortably say that my sometimes terrible

*Alf advertising his first book on his taxi. (Author's collection)*

experiences in the Second World War as an evacuee were almost from another lifetime – even though I still abhor going down the Tube!

I thought the return journey home might bring on morbid thoughts of 'popping my clogs' before seeing Newquay again. But my lovely wife, forever the realist, made the pertinent point that if we all thought in that pessimistic fashion, then it would soon encompass every single facet of our lives, even on the next round of golf! And she was spot on, as usual. Enjoy every minute of every day my friends, because none of us can see through the mirror of life.

I hope that the ex-evacuees among you have got something positive out of reading my book and that my new interpretation of the past will strike a chord with others who lived through the Second World War.

Cornwall    16.12.46

Newquay (Cornwall) land of my dreams, with superb scenery and exquisite landscape. When I was evacuated to Newquay, I spent five of the best years of my boyhood. There are five beaches in Newquay, not counting the tiny little picturesque harbour nestled against the towering cliffs. From the harbour, little fishing boats set out to sea, to catch miscellaneous fishes. They come back loaded to the capacity with fish. There is also another attraction, the countryside, quite, peaceful, not like the hurried bustling of the busy London crowds. On the outskirts of Newquay there is an aerodrome. So when I came home to London, I bid a reluctant farewell to the picturesque scene of my demi-paradise.

*Alf's first attempt at writing – at the age of eleven.*

# Also by Alf Townsend

*London Cabbie*
978-0-7509-4496-0

*Bad Lads: RAF National Service Remembered*
978-07509-4154-9

———◆———

Available from all good bookshops and direct from
The History Press

Web Orders
www.thehistorypress.co.uk

Telephone Customer Services
01453 883300